KADA & BARNEY MILLER

The Essence of YOU and ME

hachette
AUSTRALIA

Lyrics to 'Will', 'Shooting down Impossible' and 'I'll Follow' by Kada copyright © MNO Records reproduced by permission.

hachette
AUSTRALIA

Published in Australia and New Zealand in 2018
by Hachette Australia
(an imprint of Hachette Australia Pty Limited)
Level 17, 207 Kent Street, Sydney NSW 2000
www.hachette.com.au

10 9 8 7 6 5 4 3 2 1

NATIONAL
LIBRARY
OF AUSTRALIA

A catalogue record for this book is available from the National Library of Australia

ISBN: 978 0 7336 3933 3 (paperback)

Cover design by Christabella Designs
Cover photograph courtesy of Curtis Redden
Inside cover and internal photographs courtesy of authors' collection
Text design by Bookhouse, Sydney
Typeset in 12.15/19.08 pt Granjon LT Std, ITC Goudy Sans Std and Goudy Oldstyle Std
  by Bookhouse, Sydney
Printed and bound in Australia by McPherson's Printing Group

MIX
Paper from
responsible sources
FSC
www.fsc.org   FSC® C001695

The paper this book is printed on is certified against the Forest Stewardship Council® Standards. McPherson's Printing Group holds FSC® chain of custody certification SA-COC-005379. FSC® promotes environmentally responsible, socially beneficial and economically viable management of the world's forests.

In dedication to Barney's mum, Helen. Your love, strength and guidance will now live on forever through these pages, as it always will in our hearts.

And to anyone who has ever felt stuck or lost, like there is nowhere to turn, to anyone who has been told 'no' and that your dream is impossible, we hope you can find comfort, strength and your way to happiness through our story and to a life where you are free to be authentically you.

CONTENTS

'Some of us were born with the power of will;

some of us discovered it through a loss.

We were once lost souls searching for our place, but we

    were never meant to fit in.

Even in our darkest hour there is a light that follows.

Its shine seeps through the cracks just enough,

clinging to the hope that it might one day catch us.

For when they fall, they shall rise.

It's that will to carry on, to override that drives us forward

    and takes us home.'

Kada – 'Will'

YOU ARE BLESSED WITH LOVE

Love. That powerful four-letter word which is universally said every single day to describe the highest vibrational emotion one can feel towards a person or object. To us, love is the greatest gift of life. To experience love is to feel unconditional acceptance, to share each other's dreams and support each other's heartache. We have been in love for ten years. In many ways our relationship is far from normal, while in others it is just the same as any other. We have what we call an epic love: it's fiery and chaotic but within it is a beautiful order that makes it work. We are both passionate and opinionated and we tend to live in a world of pure imagination. By that we mean that we believe in every fibre of our cells that we have the ability to influence our life experience through our thoughts, choices and perception.

It hasn't always been this way. We, like many others, were once stuck in a vicious cycle of poor decisions, self-sabotage and emptiness. We soon learnt, though, that without the perfect formula of trust, honesty, forgiveness, respect and support, there would be no solid foundation for our love to stand on.

We have spent the past ten years chasing each other's dreams and experiencing each other's highs and lows. We have learnt so much about ourselves, each other and how best to grow together. When one is feeling down, the other is there to lean on. When one succeeds, we both succeed, but no amount of success, fame or fortune will ever be enough if we don't have each other to share it with.

In our lives, there have been what we call 'Wake the Eff Up' moments. These are the moments that are not in your plan. The ones that happen right when you think you're killing it at life then – BAM! – life throws a curveball. In our case, a few life-threatening, life-changing curveballs. But looking back, we now know that in each time of suffering is an opportunity to learn, grow and change the course.

One of our favourite things to do is to meet new people. We love hearing their stories and discovering what makes them who they are, and then sharing goals and celebrating the victories when they are achieved. We have always believed in the importance of building and nurturing solid relationships and surrounding ourselves with like-minded, supportive, inspiring people – and that goes for both our personal lives and in business. Our friends are quite the mixed bag, from parents to athletes to entertainers to tradesmen to servicemen to entrepreneurs. They all lead very different lives but they share something in common: they are just really good people, and they believe in us. Being kind goes a long way in life. You can really tell a lot about a person's character by the way they treat people. Is it based on what they do or who they are? We have no space in our lives for people who just can't be bothered to be nice. But to be fair, we also believe that your relationships are only as strong as the effort you put in. So, be a caring person and you will soon attract caring people into your life. That quote, 'Treat others how you want to be treated' isn't just something you say to a bully, it's a lifestyle. And at the end of the day, happiness is what we strive for, and when something no longer makes us happy we know it's time to stop and re-evaluate what it is that needs to change in order to put us back onto the path of a fulfilled life. We have learnt that when we make choices based on love, and ask ourselves, 'Is this really going to make me truly happy?' the answers are usually already within us. It's a scary thought, but it is also a very empowering one.

This is the story of our life, our love and the proof that the power of love heals, strengthens and can be the driving force behind all the magical moments in life. This is not just about romantic love, this love is found in friendships, careers, self-love and acceptance. This is living an authentic life, true to your heart's desire. This is about not taking no for an answer when all the walls are closing in on you. It's about getting back up every time you fall, and trying again. It's seeing the opportunity and the solution, not focusing on the problem. It's trusting in your intuition and ignoring the paralysing limitations that fear has put on you. It's sharing the journey with the ones you love. This is the essence of you and me.

CHAPTER 1

LOOKING BACK

BARNEY

If I were to look at my life as a road trip, I would imagine a map with two roads to the same destination. Option A is a long, straight, flat road that will get me there in less than half the time, it has five-star hotels along the way and I am guaranteed at least one upgrade. Option B has lots of mountains, roadblocks and detours, but it also potentially has the best surf along the way. Sure, Option A is probably the safe and easy choice, but it also seems like a pretty boring, predictable trip. Option B is an adventure that will be filled with many challenges and will take me well out of my comfort zone. To anyone who knows me, I'm all about Option B. Life is never a certainty and taking risks is scary, but it's also where the good shit happens.

My life has taken me through many ups and downs and I have knocked on death's door a few too many times. But with every obstacle I have found a new appreciation for life and the human body. Its ability to keep us alive every single day is pretty damn amazing. Yeah, of course I have hard days, who doesn't? But it's not because of what has happened to me. It's just that sometimes we have bad days, and that's okay. I have learnt to allow myself to just feel how I'm feeling and let it go. Because when we bottle it in, it will only turn into toxic energy, and who wants that floating around in their body? Not me.

My story started on 6 March 1979. I was born in Kempsey, New South Wales and became the sixth member of my family. It was my mum and dad, Helen and Geoff, and my two older sisters, Lara and Tania, and then me. I also had a brother, Timothy, but sadly he passed away when he was just a few hours old. He would have been the oldest of us kids.

From what I remember, I was a happy kid, full of energy, with a love for sports, animals and planes. We had moved to Temora, New South Wales, when I was two, and my first childhood best friend's name was Duncan. Our parents were friends, so it was only a matter of time before we were running amok around town together. I learnt to ride a bike when I was three, and as soon as I was confident, that was it. We would ride to each other's houses and I would ride to school. Those were the days when we didn't have to worry so much, because the people in the neighbourhood watched out for each other.

We had a dog, a Weimaraner named Aslan after the Great Lion in *The Lion, the Witch and the Wardrobe*. He was so tall that Duncan and I used to try to ride him. To this day, Duncan is a good mate of mine, and a reminder of my simple, happy early years.

Both my parents were teachers, so we moved around a lot for the first half of my childhood. Someone once told me that it is during the first seven years of life that you develop your blueprint for how you will respond to the world around you as you grow up. My first challenges in life all happened at age seven, when my parents moved us from Temora to Wellington, another country town in central west New South Wales. At the time I probably thought, *How can my parents make me leave my friends?* But then, as I grew up, I began to see the value of the lessons I learnt in those times: how to adapt to change and how to put myself out there to make new friends.

At the back of our new house was a garage with a mechanic's pit, which was ironic considering my dad was a mechanic and taught mechanics at the TAFE College. It was also the scene of my first serious injury in life. One day while my cousins were visiting, we were playing out in the garage. We thought it would be cool to put some tables on either side of the pit with a beam through the middle and jump from side to side, swinging on the metal beam. I must have done that jump a thousand times before, but on this particular day I slipped and landed in the pit on my right side, knocking myself out. I woke up in the kitchen with my whole family standing around me calling, 'David! David!' (Oh yeah, my real name is David, I'll tell you that story later. But to the world I have mostly always been Barney.) I remember sitting up and asking, 'Where am I?' but then quickly taking it back with, 'Oh no, it's okay, I know where I am,' because I heard whispers of 'ambulance', 'emergency' and 'hospital'. I think this was the first time I had really felt fear. I also didn't want to miss out on playing with my cousins, so I tried to pretend that I was okay, but unfortunately – or fortunately – for me, I didn't fool anyone. It turned out I had fractured my skull, which also led to paralysis down the right side of my face. I was transferred to a Sydney doctor and then referred to a specialist because I couldn't close my eye or eat or drink without drooling out the side of my mouth. As kids, we are kind of oblivious to the severity of many situations because adults often shield us from the reality so we can keep our free spirit alive, and this worked in my favour when it came to healing. My parents made sure to never let me think that I wouldn't recover. To me, it was just like a scratch that was waiting to scab over and would maybe leave me with a cool scar. My mind never dwelled on it as something to worry about. The hardest part about the whole situation – for me – was that I couldn't play outside for months. I felt this most at school when the bell rang each day for recess and lunch and I had to sit inside; but then the teacher, who also happened to be my mum, would let me choose someone to stay in and play with me. For some reason, kids actually wanted to do that, so it wasn't all bad.

After a while, my head and face healed and I was cleared to go back to my normal life, although my life would never really be normal again. A few months later, my parents separated. I don't remember my exact emotions. Obviously I would have been sad, but because I had moved around so much I had already learnt to adapt to change. This was a big change, though. One day there were five of us living together as one big happy family and the next, my dad moved into an apartment on the other side of town and my eldest sister, Lara, was at boarding school. So, then there were just the three of us: Mum, Tania and me. All I knew in that moment was that I was officially the man of the house.

After two years in Wellington, there was more change. My dad had moved to Sydney, and my mum and I moved again, this time to South West Rocks after she got a new job teaching at St Joseph's Primary in Kempsey. Lara moved to Newcastle to start university and my other sister, Tania, went to boarding school in Grafton so now it was just Mum and me living in the holiday apartment my family had owned most of my life. This time round, I was excited for the move, because South West Rocks was the place we had spent every Christmas holidays since I was a baby. It was where I discovered my love for the ocean and where I was introduced to surfing. We had family friends, the Hassetts, who lived in the area, and their three sons, Tim, Mick and Johnny, were all surfers. They were my first idols. I remember desperately wanting to be out the back in the surf with them but instead I would play with my bodyboard on the shoreline, but then I would instinctively stand up and pretend I was ripping like them. Moving to the coast had been a dream come true, but I could only go to the beach on weekends because I went to school in Kempsey, which back then was a half-an-hour drive inland. We had moved during the Christmas holidays, just in time for me to start Year 5. My mum was the Year 3 teacher at the school, so we would drive together every day. We would talk about my goals and hobbies, and though I was really into soccer and cricket, surfing was quickly becoming my main obsession. I would often sit on the beach and watch the surfers out the back, studying their moves. I loved seeing how stoked they were when they came in from a sick surf session, and I wanted to experience that feeling. My mum still wasn't confident enough in my ability to get out the back without any help, though, so she bought me a skateboard in the hope that I would stop pestering her every day to let me go. I would spend hours skating, imagining waves beneath me. I also joined the surf club and local swimming club so I could strengthen my competence – and my confidence – in the water. Before my swimming carnivals Mum would always give me a kiss and say, 'Swim like a shark is chasing you.' As funny as it may seem, it worked. Those motivational words had got me the eight- and nine-age champion medals, back in Wellington. Then through to my athletics carnivals, she would again kiss me on the forehead and say, 'Run like a lion is chasing you.'

Again I became the eight- and nine-age champion in athletics too. My mum was always my biggest supporter and it became something we bonded over: setting goals and then working out strategies to reach them. I would definitely say that this is the source of all my strength: my mum. My fearless ambitions in athletics and adventure, though, is from my dad. Everything from roller-coasters to car races to my first introductions to the ocean. My dad always made me feel safe and never afraid to try.

When I was ten, my mum finally agreed to let me head out into the ocean by myself. When the Hassett boys came to pick me up for my first real surf session, every emotion was running through my body, from fear to pure froth. They had all been surfing for years, so my mum trusted that I would be in safe hands. We arrived at a surf spot called The Gap, and as I stood on the shore to strap my leggy to my right ankle I saw them all putting theirs on their left; I felt a little bummed that they were goofy footers and I was a natural, but then they told me that that year's world number one surfer, Tom Curren, was also a natural, so then I was pretty stoked. I hopped on the board – a second-hand blue five foot five inch Raw Energy by Simon Anderson that my mum had just bought me – and paddled out for the first time. Before this moment, I had never left the whitewash close to the shore and had never known the feeling of paddling. It was scary and loud and I was thrashed all over the place as I followed the boys, pushing our way through the waves. I was suddenly grateful for my few years of swimming training but my little arms still tired quickly, but the pure joy and adrenalin I felt overrode any sense of struggle. When I finally made it out the back the boys cheered and high-fived me, and I felt the greatest sense of pride and accomplishment I had ever known.

Back then, it was a teach-yourself kind of sport. We didn't have the luxury of having someone pushing us onto waves like the groms today. It was a sink-or-swim mentality and you either could do it or you couldn't, and if you couldn't you just practised every day until you could and then practised some more to get better. Not many of our parents surfed so this was the way to learn back then. I wish they'd had the surf programs they have now when I was learning. I would have been out there so much more.

Once you get past the waves, there is a calm, peaceful energy; it's hard to describe because it's like nothing else I have experienced. I still remember that first time, even though I didn't have long to take it all in, because a wave appeared and the boys called me onto it. All I could hear was, 'Paddle, paddle, paddle! Stand up, stand up!' Then as the wave picked me up I jumped to my feet and rode it till it faded out. Instantly I had a new sense of freedom, almost as if I was flying.

From that moment on all I could think about was surfing. I suddenly had a whole new appreciation for the ocean and could finally feel for myself why the Hassett boys lived and breathed it.

That Christmas all I wanted was surf everything. I got a Rip Curl wetsuit, and my first surf videos – the *1989 Quiksilver*

Eddie Aikau Big Wave Invitational and *Kelly Slater in Black and White* – which opened my eyes to professional surfing, and the hunger began.

As much as I loved my home and my life, when my mum told me she had received an offer for vice principal of a new school, in a new town, I felt okay about it. 'As long as there's an ocean with surf,' I told her, 'then I can be happy anywhere.' That was until we visited our new home – Sawtell – and spent the day looking at houses. The moment I saw the beach, I hoped this would be our home forever. It just felt like home, more so than any of the other places we had lived. We sold the apartment in South West Rocks that had been a part of my entire life, packed up everything and said our farewells. Luckily we were moving only an hour away, so it wasn't goodbye forever.

We moved into our new home and I was enrolled to start Year 8 the following month. For the rest of the summer holidays, I spent every day on the beach, getting to know the waves and making friends with the locals. Mum would drop me off in the morning and pick me up after lunch. I often thought to myself: *How could life get any better than this?*

CHAPTER 2

KATHRYN WITH A K

KADA

Someone once asked me, what is my greatest asset. Most people value their worth in terms of objects they own, but for me, my greatest asset is my imagination. My freedom of thought. My ability to think outside the box and create something beautiful out of nothing. To be able to express the feelings I experience, through my stories and songs. To see the big picture when it makes no sense to others. To show empathy and kindness, through imagining the lives others endure. I have always been this way; always lived in a world of pure imagination. Though it wasn't long ago, it is hard to remember life without technology to help occupy our time.

When I was a child, my favourite games – the ones at which I excelled – were based in imagination. Why is it that when we grow up we tend to lose this playful and creative side of ourselves? Why are we so afraid to share our wonderful, crazy, wild ideals of life? Are we ashamed to be different, or are we just conditioned to fit into society, even if it means losing a piece of our unique self along the way? These have been the questions on my mind for some time now. They say when you are lost or stuck, then the best thing to do is to go back, retrace your steps to the beginning or till you last felt safe, and start again. I have found that the core things in life that matter to me now and the lifestyle to which I am attracted, are from elements of my childhood that brought me the most happiness. Have you noticed that our favourite songs growing up stay with us forever? Years later, when we hear them played we are teleported to that exact memory and all those same feelings come flooding back in. A lot of my favourite childhood films are now being re-created, and it has been amazing to relive them all over again in a brand-new way. The feeling I get from these memories is so intoxicatingly pure and rich, filled with hope, love and endless possibilities. This is the happiness I now crave and strive to replicate every day in everything I do. When we align ourselves with our core values, there is no reason every moment can't be bliss. I have often asked myself: 'If I had known then what I know now, would things have been different?' The answer is probably no. I believe I am where I am today, and hold the knowledge that I hold, because I have hit rock bottom and had to climb my way back up that bitch of a mountain. I can now honestly say that I have no regrets, and only now do I understand that every choice has led me to this wonderful moment where I can share the story of a little girl with big dreams and an even bigger heart. Who lost her way and then after almost losing herself completely, found it again when she allowed herself to experience love again. This is where my story begins.

I was born, Kathryn Maree Beaton – my mother's maiden name. Neither Barney nor I go by our given names. I even now go by two, Kate and Kada, but you will learn more about this throughout the story. I grew up in a small country town in the central west of New South Wales called Cowra. On 10 January 1990 in the local hospital located on the top of the hill, my grandma, Cynthia, was there to welcome me into the world with my new mum, Sharron. My mum was not long seventeen, and I'm sure this was the scariest moment of her life but she had decided to keep me, despite all the fears that probably consumed her. I'm sure her initial thoughts were focused on how she would care for and raise a baby when she wasn't fully a woman yet, but all those doubts were taken away the moment she held me in her arms. Her life finally held purpose and I was hers, forever.

At the time of my birth, I didn't have a dad present, but I was already surrounded by unconditional love. I had thick, dark hair and a dark complexion that I had obviously inherited from my biological Polynesian father, because my mum was white-skinned with sandy blonde hair. They met when my mum lived in Tonga with her family. To this day I have still never met him but I am grateful for him giving me life.

After I was born my mum reconnected with her childhood sweetheart, Jason, who also happens to be the big brother of her best friend. He had heard of Mum's pregnancy and was secretly trying to send her money to help out, but because he never actually made contact over the first few months, my mum was convinced he didn't like her anymore. The romantic truth was that he had never stopped loving her but he didn't want to start something until he was sure it was what they both wanted. After all, it was more than just the two of them; I was a part of the package. Of course, though, I had him wrapped around my tiny finger from the moment he held me and that was it, he was my dad and I became Kathryn Southwell.

My dad's pride and joy was his Holden Commodore. He had worked so hard to save up for it but as soon as I was in the picture, so was a baby seat. My mum says that's how she knew it was true love. Two years later my parents got married and I was the flower girl. They have been happily married for twenty-five years and are still very much in love.

We moved into a little two-bedroom shack behind my dad's work. He was the manager of a hardware store, and my mum was my full-time mummy. Our days were spent playing at the park and reading books – my favourite was *Snow White and the Seven Dwarfs*, which my nanno gave me for my third birthday and I must have made my mum read it to me a thousand times. Every afternoon I would count down the hours till my dad returned home from work so we could sing and dance together. That was always my favourite part of the day.

After a couple of years we moved around the corner to a bigger house and it is this home that holds some of my most treasured memories. I lived there from age four to eight, in those magical years when our true, authentic selves can steer our thoughts. Out the back was an old two-storey cubbyhouse with a slippery dip. It was a dream for my imagination and where I developed my love for hosting parties, although my guests were usually my imaginary friend, Amie, or my porcelain dolls. I would spend hours creating the scenes I would live in for the afternoon. Every detail was accounted for in my mind, and to me it was all I needed to have fun.

That was until my new baby sister arrived into my world. Rachael was chubby and bubbly and she was my new best friend. I remember wanting to play with her every second of the day, so I would purposely speak with a high-pitched squealing voice in the hope that she would wake up from her nap. Unfortunately this also happened to be close to my everyday voice, so she very quickly became immune to the excitable high-volume chatter that came out of my mouth, maybe even soothed by it. Thursdays were our favourite day of the week, because it was the grocery-shop day and Mum would treat us with a packet of our favourite chips. I always chose Light 'n' Tangy and Rachael would have Chicken. I loved to practise my performing skills while we were out. I would stand at the front of the moving shopping trolley as if I were the star of a hit Broadway show, singing at the top of my voice to anyone who walked past. My set list was usually a mixture of Disney classics and songs I'd either made up or learnt in Sunday School. The beautiful thing about being young is that you don't need permission to express the way you feel: if you're happy, you laugh hysterically; if you're sad, you cry without any thoughts of judgement; when you're angry, you throw the biggest tantrum you can whenever and wherever you like with full commitment. We often like to categorise kids as either naughty or well behaved but the truth is, with some exceptions, they are usually just kids expressing themselves, and I often hope they hold onto that free spirit for as long as possible, because it's heartbreaking when that confidence in self-expression starts to fade away as they grow up and integrate with their peers. As a child, there is no shame in telling somebody our likes and dislikes, because our intentions are honest and pure.

When I turned six, my parents enrolled me in classical piano lessons with Mrs Hazel Winkley. She had lovely silver hair and dressed with a quirky sophistication. Her lips were always stained pink. She lived on the outskirts of town in a beautiful brick home with lush manicured gardens. I loved playing in the garden chasing butterflies and humming the tunes of that week's piano piece as I waited for my lesson.

When I was seven, my dad came home from work and told us he had a surprise for us. We all jumped in the car with so much excitement, anxiously waiting to see where he was driving us to. We arrived on a property on the other side of town on the road that leads out to Wyangala Dam. When we made the turn onto the road, I was sure Dad was taking us to the waterslides but also a little confused because we weren't wearing our swimmers. I wondered if Mum had sneakily packed a bag in the back of the car, but when the car came to a complete stop nowhere near the slides, we were greeted by a playful golden labrador. 'Her name is Mindy and she's your new pet,' said the nice man. Without even really having a moment to process the words, Rachael and I pounced out of the car to hug our newest family member. I had begged for a dog for so long and could not believe that my wish had finally come true. She was eighteen months old and full of life. Her previous owner didn't have the time that she needed to burn off her endless energy. Luckily, Rachael and I had exactly that. We spent hours outside trying to teach her tricks and playing fetch with the oranges from the tree in the backyard. Anyone who has owned a labrador knows that they are mischievously clever. She had a bad habit of digging and chewing up shoes, hoses and anything that was worth anything and had been left outside, which seemed to be a lot of my toys. This got her in trouble on a regular basis, but the moment she would come to smother us in slobbery kisses, she was always forgiven.

Our house was a few blocks away from my school. My two best friends, Erin and Kiara, lived on the way, so in the mornings my mum would walk me to the end of my street to meet my friends and then the three of us would walk down the laneway behind their houses, which led directly to the school. This was my first taste of independence. We all met in preschool and bonded over our love for music. We all shared dreams of becoming the next Spice Girls and travelling the world singing to our millions of fans. Erin's house was on a busy main road with a huge verandah out the front. We used to love playing dress-ups in her big sister's closet and raiding her mum's make-up stash to get our looks on point. After an hour of glamour, it was time to take to the verandah stage and sing to the streets of Cowra. Of course, every time we made the mistake of taking too long to get ready, we ended up with only ten minutes left before I had to go home. But it was enough time to make us fall in love with the exhilarating feeling of performing. We later decided to expand our group and invited a few new members to perform with us on our classroom tour, during which our show consisted of anything including Spice Girls, Janet Jackson, Britney Spears and Steps.

A lot of precious memories were made while I lived in that house near Erin's, but it was time to move on because we had welcomed our newest baby sister, Clarissa. Our new home was in a quiet cul de sac on the other side of town. I remember it being really old and small when we first moved in but over a few years my dad gutted, rebuilt and extended it from two bedrooms to a six-bedroom home. It was on a large block with a vacant lot next door, and my dad had made an agreement with the land owner to put some sheep on the property to help keep the grass down. On the back left side of our block we built a chicken coop and kept a variety of hens and a rooster. This was the home where I was first taught responsibility. We built a big veggie garden at the back of the block and my dad made me a deal: if I looked after the strawberries, I could sell them and keep the money. Excited at the chance to become 'rich', I agreed to the deal and started digging away. I have to say, I was not really the gardening type, but when my strawberries were ready to harvest, I packed them into punnets and made my first sales at my dad's work. There were a lot of great lessons to learn in the way we were brought up, especially to nurture, respect and give thanks to the hands that provide the food we eat. At the time I didn't fully appreciate this sustainable and organic way of living; I just wanted to fit in and shop at the supermarket like everybody else – none of my friends had to pick their own veggies out of the garden every day, or collect the chicken eggs while dodging a psychotic rooster, or fill and filter the rain water from the tanks. It's almost ironic that this is one of those elements of my childhood that I now crave in my life and so desperately want to replicate in my own home. I also now take pride in knowing that out of necessity and affordability, my parents chose a path that could not only feed us but could also teach us the ethical foundations of the circle of life.

CHAPTER 3

BARNEY AND FRIENDS

BARNEY

There is a lot to say about a person by the company they keep. Growing up, I was taught that to make great friends you have to be a great friend. I actually learnt a lot about true friendship from my pets. If there is a dog in my radius, it won't be long before I zone in on it and lose focus on everything else around me. I love to just sit and admire their simple yet purposeful way of life. I was fortunate to grow up surrounded by animals. Our first dog's name was Milo. He was a Kelpie with high energy who loved to go on adventures and loved the chase, specifically cars. After he had escaped multiple times, my family made the tough decision to give him to a new family on a farm where he was free to run and chase things all day long. Next was my sister Tania's Weimaraner, Aslan. He was the first pet allowed in the house, so he really became a part of our family. Aslan was so patient and would let me lie all over him. It was one of the saddest moments of my life when he passed away after he was hit by a car, having had just a few short years with him. It was one of those hard life lessons in dealing with the pain of loss.

When we eventually made the move to Sawtell, after a few years in South West Rocks without a pet, I requested a puppy. I had missed having a pet to come home to and felt it was time to liven up the house a bit because it was just my mum and me. Dogs weren't allowed on our property, though, so Mum took me into the RSPCA to choose a cat. There was a new litter of tabby kittens tumbling around on the floor in one of the cages. I climbed in to sit on the floor but before I even made it to the ground I was pounced on and clawed by little balls of fur. That's when I saw him – the coolest cat of the litter. He was a mixture of black, grey and white, his fur thick and fluffy with a bushy tail. And that was it: I had chosen my new friend and I named him Rusty. As I sat and played with Rusty, I chatted to the workers about my love of animals and how I desperately also wanted a dog. They told me about their volunteer program, and I jumped at the opportunity, signing up straightaway. From then on, in my spare time that summer, when I wasn't surfing I was at the RSPCA hanging with the dogs. I remember at one stage taking eight or nine of them out of their cages at once and letting them run wild and play together in the outside park. The best part of the job was bringing as much joy into their lives as they did to mine. The worst was having to leave them there, not knowing if they would ever find a home of their own.

Soon summer came to an end and it was time for me to start at my new school. My first day was a bit of a blur. This was the biggest school I had ever been to and it was pretty overwhelming. It was also a different school structure from what I was used to. Having to learn which class was in what block or room number was a task in itself. Of course I misplaced my map and, being a typical teenage boy, instead of going to the office to get a new one, I just fumbled my way around until I got my bearings. Fortunately I had already made a few friends over the summer, which helped make the transition a bit easier. At this stage I was still known as my given name, David, but everyone knows Aussies can never call someone their real name; everyone has a nickname and mine became Barney Miller after the '70s detective show. A boy at school called me it one day and, just like that, it stuck. I went through school with teachers not even realising my real name was David.

Over the summer I had seen a group of four brothers at the beach every day. They were the Webber boys and they lived right on the beach. Ryan, Luke and Toby were surfers and the youngest, Leigh, was a bodyboarder. They had caught my attention because they used to all wear white helmets in the surf after a friend of theirs was knocked unconscious by his board at the beginning of the Christmas holidays. The board had gashed his head open and he ended up with a steel plate in it. That hasn't stopped him though, and to this day he is still the first one out and the last one in. Every day I would see the Webber brothers in the surf, ripping past me and then disappearing into the dunes, up their private track to their house. I remember thinking it would be so cool to live that close to the beach. I always imagined that one day I would.

One afternoon I was walking past the Webbers' house and started chatting to the boys. It didn't take long for Toby and me to become best mates and the Webbers to become my second family. We were in the surf together every day, and after the surf we would race each other up the track starving. After raiding the cupboards we would always turn to the old faithful – toast – eating as much as we could fit into our stomachs. This soon led to toast-eating competitions. It started with who could eat their piece the fastest; then we upped the stakes to eating no-hands off our plates; and then we took it outside, tying the toast to the clothes line and challenging each other to eat with no hands, and if the string broke and the toast fell, we would still have to eat it off the ground to win. Our friendship was definitely competitive right from the get go, but that's what made it awesome. Being the youngest and only boy growing up, I loved being surrounded by a family of boys; I had people to competitively motivate and push me to be the best in whatever I set out to do. It was a first-in, fight-for-survival mentality in their household and one I learnt to adapt to very quickly – otherwise I would have literally starved.

The only time I was detached from my board or the Webbers was when I would visit my dad in Sydney for a week every school holidays. My dad and I always shared a love of sports. From a young age, he got me into soccer, mini ball (which is kids' basketball with a lower ring) and tennis. Tennis was one that stuck right through to my late teenage years; I competed every Saturday morning. The thing I loved about tennis was that, like surfing, it could be a solo sport. I loved being in that mental space of taking the responsibility on myself and not having to depend on somebody else to help carry the game. Whether I won or lost, it was all up to me.

One of the best things about living in Sawtell was becoming part of its surfing community. I joined the Sawtell Boardriders Club, which became my introduction to competitive surfing, and I loved it. There is something so satisfying about putting on a rashie and competing. I believe that it's in these situations that our true personalities shine through. You're either a mongrel or you're not. Me, I'm a pure-bred mongrel for sure. I live for the challenge, to do whatever it takes to improve on where I was yesterday.

One Friday afternoon my mum came home from work with some big news: a house one block back from the beach had just come onto the market. It was an old two-bedroom shack 100 metres from the beach, a two-minute walk from the main street – and to top it off, it was only a few houses up the road from the Webbers. It wasn't much to look at – a real fixer-upper – but we could see the potential, and the lifestyle we had been dreaming of outweighed the work needed. Mum put in an offer and we waited anxiously for the next week for an answer. When the call came in to say our offer was accepted I felt like I had literally hit the jackpot. It's a surfer's dream to live that close to the surf, and I couldn't believe I was one of the lucky ones.

The timing couldn't have been more perfect. I had been getting into a bit of trouble at school for ditching class to go surfing, and I had started to fall behind in my studies. The last straw had come when I was suspended for drinking alcohol at a school social. The fact that my mum was the vice principal at another local school didn't help. It was towards the end of Year 11 and everybody was getting ready to start their final year of high school. That wasn't going to be me though, from too many days missed and assignments unfinished, I was given the ultimatum: repeat Year 11 or be expelled. Those words rang in my ears for a while. Not because I was bummed I had to repeat but because I knew how disappointed my parents were going to be in me. Repeating a year was the easy part. Toby Webber and a bunch of my mates were in the year below, so that meant we would graduate together, so secretly I was stoked! Telling my dad wasn't the best conversation we've had. He was the principal of a TAFE College in Sydney, so it wasn't his proudest moment either, I'm sure. But after a lot of lectures and discussions, I agreed to take my education more seriously. I wasn't skipping school because

I hated it or just for the sake of it; it was mostly because my obsession with surfing ran so deep. It was my sanity, and when I was away from the water for even a day, I felt myself losing focus; all I could think about was what the waves were like. Moving to the beach gave me the freedom to surf before and after school, as long as I kept up my grades.

We finally had a house with a yard, and after convincing Mum to let me bring home a puppy, my adventures with Kirra the mischievously clever beagle started. She was without a doubt the cutest thing I had ever seen. Kirra taught me the true meaning of patience, loyalty and unconditional love, and she sure did test how far she could push them every day. But beyond her misunderstood naughty behaviour and her sometimes inconvenient food addictions, we were buddies, the best of buds, and she was there for me through some of the hardest moments of my life.

Monday nights for the previous few years had been booked for dinner at the Greenwells' house. My mum had met Mal Greenwell, who was also divorced, a few years prior and they had become great friends. Over the years spent together they became closer and fell in love; I could see how much Mal loved my mum, and it was so good to see her so happy again. Mal had five daughters, Sarah, Jesi, Hannah, Claire and Bonnie, and a son, Tom, who was a year younger than me. At Christmas time when my two older sisters were also home we were like the modern-day turbo-charged Brady Bunch.

Round two of Year 11 was proving to be a great idea. I had a solid group of mates and our school hangout spot was out the front of the chapel in a little undercover area. This is where The Chapel Boys came to life. The group consisted of me, Toby, Tommy O, Track, Farry, Matt, Scotty, Trent and Peaz (Leigh Webber). The perks of repeating a year meant that I went from being one of the youngest of my year, to one of the oldest of my year. I was the first of my friends to get my licence. I'd borrow my mum's car on weekends and take the boys on surf trips up and down the coast. It was a blue '91 Nissan Pulsar with roof racks, and once we all had that taste of independence and freedom, we were ready to take on the world.

* * *

Once I put my head down and gave my schooling a real go, it turned out I was kind of smart, especially at maths. I was gaining momentum and even managed to get voted in as Sports Captain for my house. I was pretty stoked I led my house to its first win in both the swimming and athletics carnivals in years. Another bonus of the repeated year in school was an extra trip to the slopes for the annual ski trip. After four years on skis I tried snowboarding and realised that it was so much more fun and had me wondering why I hadn't tried it sooner.

Some of my all-time favourite memories and stories come from my second year of Year 11 and Year 12. They are the stories that still leave me rolling around in laughter whenever I reminisce with anyone who was part of that epic time of life. Like the time I joined the Rock Eisteddfod with a mate. Everyone mocked us for learning to dance, but imagine being two young lads in a dressing room with hundreds of girls getting dressed around you for the competition. What's weird about that? I even landed the lead male role as Zeus in the performance of *Pandora's Box*. Well, Zeus wears a toga with a split down the front, and me not being a big fan of underwear had to resort to wearing a pair of white undies belonging to my friend Cara. Not the comfiest, but I guess it was better than letting it all hang out.

I was approached by a mate to join the new AFL team they were building at the school to compete in the Commonwealth Bank Cup, which would have us playing against all the schools in the surrounding areas. I knew nothing about the sport but was always keen to give anything a crack. I soon discovered I loved the game, and our team ended up winning the Cup. Marto was the team coach and very quickly became like a big brother to me. He later recruited me to play representative AFL for the Sawtell Saints Club, and it fed into my competitive edge. The game was fast and took quick-thinking action to pull off a win. There was something so exciting about being able to shepherd your teammate and take out anyone who came for him while he had the ball. It tested my fitness and strength in a whole new way but also gave me confidence in my ability to push through when the odds were stacked against me.

Repeating a year of school gave me a new outlook on my life. It was a good lesson in taking responsibility for my actions and made me realise that even if you mess up, you can always go back, re-evaluate your attitude and make a change. It was also my first experience in the importance of the people you surround yourself with and how they can play a major role in the way you approach things. It was in that time I made some of my best mates, most of whom are, thankfully, still in my life today.

CHAPTER 4

GROWING PAINS

KADA

I think it's safe to say that at one point or another everybody has felt the desire to be 'normal' and fit in. I was, and still am at times, no exception to that, but what is normal anyway? What is it that makes us want to hide our true self in the hope of tasting the feeling of acceptance? I think it really comes down to self-love, self-acceptance and inner confidence. I had all of these things until about Year 4 of primary school. I can remember the exact moment that it began to be stripped away from me. I grew up in a Christian home, and everyone I was surrounded by outside of school was of the same strong belief system. My heart was filled with pure love and kindness, and my expectation of the world was that it was the same. Treat others how you want to be treated, was a moral that I lived by but unfortunately others weren't always taught this. My first experience of bullying started when I joined the school choir and wanted to try out for a solo part. I didn't get it because the solos were only ever given to seniors, but later that day I started to hear whispers of classmates making fun of me; 'Wow, she must think she's so good that she could get a solo over a senior!' The thing is, at that stage I still held a confidence in myself, so I fought back with, 'Well, yes, actually. I *am* good enough to take that solo over a senior but I was never given the chance to audition.' In that moment laughter echoed around the room and as a piece of my soul was crushed, for the first time I experienced self-doubt. From then it went to teasing and torment about my family's beliefs, the fact that the colour of my skin was different from the rest of my family, and that I didn't wear branded clothing. I could feel myself little by little conforming to what I thought my peers would like more and even found myself standing in silence when others became the new targets. I would go home feeling guilty and dirty at the thought that I wanted to be like these people. The truth is I didn't really, but ever since I can remember I have had a fear of people disliking me, so I just played by the rules.

Every Easter holidays my family would drive to Coffs Harbour – a trip that would normally take ten hours but took us closer to fifteen due to my chronic car sickness. It was 1999 and just like every year, the Easter long weekend was wet. Our local church belonged to a collective of churches around Australia and it was the annual Easter convention. It was my favourite time of year because we got to go to the beach and I saw my friends and their families from the other churches. Every year I looked forward to the musical acts and couldn't wait for the day I could get up and perform too.

We arrived at the church for the Saturday morning service to the news that a member of the church's son had been in a car accident. Another boy was trapped in the car in a critical condition and they weren't sure if he would make it. The church was asked to pray for the two boys, and for some strange reason I felt really attached and connected to the incident. I prayed for the boy who was fighting for his life, that he would make it through and go on to live a happy life. I think this may have been the first incident I had heard of somebody nearly dying and even though I had never met either boy, I knew the family of one, and all of a sudden I saw myself in their position and was taught the meaning of mortality in its truest form.

We returned home from our holiday in Coffs and from what was supposed to be a life-changing experience, but the joy was quickly erased when school started again. It didn't take me long to go back to being a follower and reverting to my insecurities. When I tried to tell my friends about my holiday they didn't seem interested, so I remember blurting out the most absurd story that kind of came out before I even knew what I was saying. I told my friends that we travelled in a bus that drives itself. *What?!* Why would I even say that? I remember the looks on their faces, it was like they actually thought I may have been crazy. I stood there for a few seconds in deep regret hoping that nobody heard me; and then came the laughter. I then had no choice but to laugh and say, 'Just kidding, but one day we will I'm sure.' What I would have given to take those words back in that moment. If I were to say it today, it might not be a crazy scenario, I was just eighteen years ahead of the game. I can't tell you exactly what it was that made me feel like I had to make up these stories to fit in but as each day passed the pressure grew and it was beginning to cloud my judgement.

When I started high school my need to be known and popular only grew. I was finally the one being noticed by the boys, not only in my grade but in the ones above, and I loved the attention. Because all the local primary schools integrated into one high school, I suddenly had a tonne of new friends and I felt like I was finally gaining back confidence. Underneath though, I was still always terrified of it all being taken away. That's the thing about reputation, it doesn't matter how good it is; you do one thing against the grain and it can be the end of your glory days. Every day I woke up and put on my face. I hid behind a smile pretending that everything came easily to me but little did they all know how much work it was to keep up appearances. I pretty much lived a double life from the day I started high school. I had church every weekend, so I would make up excuses why I couldn't go to a party or commit to playing representative netball. From there lying became pretty much second nature; I hated disappointing people, so I just told them what they wanted to hear.

I wish I'd known back then that I was not the only person feeling this way, that everyone goes through their own form of insecurities. I'm sure it would have been comforting to know that I wasn't alone in it all and that it does in fact get better, but in saying that I also accept this is one of life's great lessons.

Growing up in a small town can be tough. Everyone thinks they know everyone else's story, but really they know nothing. They see the side that is put forward for the public, but they don't see the struggle beneath it. Having friends you can trust can really make a difference through those hard times. I was part of a big friendship circle but my closest friends were Gemma, Monique, Lyndall and Lisa. Gem was a beam of love, and friends with everyone. We bonded over our love of music, and whenever we were together we would write songs and harmonise to our favourites. Mon was a naturally stunning girl and had a beautiful soul to match. We were true soul sisters and all of my favourite memories from my teenage years include her. Lyndall was that incredible friend with whom you could spend every second and never get sick of and never fight with. She wasn't afraid of being different and trying new things, which made every experience with her so much fun. Lisa was practically family. Her Uncle Donald married my Aunty Nicole. We were in the same roll-call class and every morning we would share secrets through notes we passed to each other. If there was anything new in my life – such as a boy I liked, someone I didn't like or just basic gossip – Lisa would be the first to hear about it. A lot of my dilemmas at school were solved through our morning chats. One thing I always prided myself on was that I didn't belong to a particular group and loved to hop between different friends during recess and lunch. It kept me stimulated and inspired but also helped keep me out of the everyday drama.

On my first day of high school I met two seniors, Drew and Steve. We became friends and they watched out for me around school. Drew had the ability to make me want to tell him all my secrets even though I knew he probably wouldn't keep any of them; he wouldn't tell people in order to start rumours, he would almost trick me into saying it out loud myself. He was big on facing your fears and always told me if you want something, don't talk about it in secret – go and get it. Our friendship grew when I started working with him at Eagle Boys Pizza. I hated wearing the uniform hat because it messed up my hair so I would sometimes purposely 'forget' it, only to have Drew conveniently always have a spare one in his car. He would think it was hilarious as I put it on my head with a scowl and eye roll.

Music and English were my two favourite classes, and they gave me the tools to grow as a singer and a writer. At the end of each term we held a music night to showcase our work, and after I performed my first ever solo performance of Jewel's 'Foolish Games', the school's vice principal became a huge supporter of mine and believed in my ability to pursue a career in music. He also knew how easy it is to let the opinions of others sway your choices, so to help with my stage presence and to fight off performance anxiety he asked me to be the official singer for the national anthem at every school assembly. Performing in front of your peers is probably as scary as it gets, so if I could perfect that, I could perform anywhere. The first time was pretty nerve racking. The seating of the hall was charted by roll call, so because my last name started with an S my seat was up towards the back. As the end of the assembly approached I got up out of my seat, squeezed my way past everyone in my row and made my way to the stage. 'Deep breaths, you were born for this,' I repeated to myself as my hands went clammy and I felt like I needed to pee. As I walked up the stairs to the stage I tried not to make eye contact with anyone, and then someone in the crowd gave a wolf whistle and it was like a switch turned on inside me. I opened my eyes and looked out to the entire school of students and teachers standing up waiting for me to lead them through the anthem. The piano started and I began to sing. At the end, a roar of applause came from the ground before me. Approval. I had found my place in the school and it was like I could finally breathe. They liked a part of me that wasn't fake and that didn't have to try too hard because it was a true piece of me. The most genuine piece of me.

From that point on, things went well, though I was still juggling my two identities: the good Christian girl to my family, and the fun party girl to my friends. My parents were doing the best they could to keep me on the right path but at times it felt like I was being suffocated. For the first time I was seeing the world for what it really was and I wanted to make my choices based on my experiences rather than what I had always been told. Because my mum and dad were young, their parenting decisions were heavily influenced by the opinions and judgement of the church, which focused on fear rather than trust. I was so torn between wanting to be part of all the fun things my friends were doing and pleasing my family and the people of the church, that it just became easier to hide things from my parents. I think that's sometimes the thing with religion: we get so caught up in the beliefs that we forget why we have them in the first place and misinterpret the core meaning behind it all.

As I grow older I am better able to look at this time in my life from my parents' perspective. I have been told that being the father of a daughter is, on one hand, the greatest joy in the world, but on the other, the most terrifying. There is such a strong, innate need to protect her from anything that could hurt her. There is no denying my dad's love for me. When I was about eight he asked me if I would be okay with him adopting me, which would make him my legal father. I remember my parents making a big deal about it, my poor dad was probably so nervous to talk to me about it, but I was like, 'Yeah, okay cool, can I play now . . .' I guess because I had only ever known him as my dad I didn't see the importance of what he was asking. Little did I know that he was also working two jobs to save up the money to pay for the adoption. I think the most beautiful thing about my relationship with my dad is knowing that he chose to love me, despite the fact I have tested that love in more ways than I am proud of. He has also seen me through some of my toughest times and still, no matter what, proudly calls me his daughter.

* * *

It was the morning of 6 March 2004 and I woke up at my friend Lyndall's house to my phone ringing. It was my dad, and my immediate reaction was to wonder why he was calling me at seven o'clock on a Saturday morning. On the other end of the phone, Dad was asking if I had spoken to my friend Drew and when was the last time I had seen him. I was still half-asleep and replied, 'Tuesday, when he dropped me home from work.' The next words that came through the phone were the last ones I ever thought I would hear. 'Sweetie, I've just been told that last night Drew took his life. He's dead.' I instantly dropped the phone and everything went into slow motion, and then stopped. A few seconds passed and I picked up the phone to hear my dad repeating the same words. I was in shock and just kept telling him that there must have been a mistake. 'I have his hat,' I told my dad, 'I'm giving it back to him on Tuesday.' I had never experienced anything like this before, so I was a bit all over the place. I was in denial, sure that I would see him the following week and everything would be the same as it had always been. I went to netball that afternoon and still no tears, even when people sought me out to ask if I had heard the news and if I was okay; I just blocked it out. I couldn't bring myself to say the words out loud, that he was really gone and I would never talk to him again. Later that night I spoke to my Aunty Jess who had been great friends with Drew and his twin brother Rory since primary school – hearing her voice was what finally broke me. I was fourteen years old and witnessing first-hand the devastating result of silent depression. On the outside, Drew had it all, but we will never know what it was like inside his mind and his heart. I just wish he could have seen the number of people who turned up to his funeral to celebrate his life and mourn the loss of him. I wish he knew how loved he was and how missed he would be. That day changed my life; that day broke my heart for the first time.

Less than a week after Drew's death, my Uncle Nathan, who was practically my big brother, was in a car accident. He was airlifted to Sydney where he was in and out of sedated consciousness in ICU after suffering cardiac arrest and having multiple emergency surgeries. Thankfully he survived and had no permanent injuries, but the thought of losing him too was beginning to overwhelm me. It hurt so much that I didn't really know how to process it, and my heart felt numb. I was grateful to be alive and well but I couldn't shake the feeling that it wasn't the end of this horrible emotional roller-coaster.

After a few months had passed, things were starting to feel a little closer to normal again. I rode the bus to school most mornings, and this day was meant to be just like every other day. A girl on the bus asked if I had heard the news. 'What news?' 'Gav committed suicide last night.' Gav was like a big teddy bear. One of the kindest souls I had ever met. I would sit with him every recess for a few minutes jamming out to whatever was playing in his headphones. Nine times out of ten it was Tupac. He introduced me to the world of R'n'B and hip hop, and then on the opposite end of the scale we shared a love of country music. He was loved by all who knew him but liked to keep to himself a lot. In hindsight I have questioned whether I saw a sign of his struggle or if there was anything that could have been said to make him want to stay. Losing Gav and the days to follow were some of the hardest times I have had. I found it difficult just to get back on with my life. Everyone around me was sad and though I tried to be strong I struggled to deal with my feelings of sorrow, anger and confusion. It was affecting my school work weeks later and that made me feel weak. But really, how do we control grief? What is an appropriate time to let go and move on? Generally it's not something we are taught to cope with. I had this warped idea that I couldn't express how I was really feeling. That it would draw too much attention or make me look less than appealing. I remember feeling trapped in my emotions, not knowing how to communicate the way I felt to my friends and my parents while trying to shield my sisters from the reality of life. I felt like my pain was less important than that of others who were closer to Gav and Drew, not knowing that I had every right to miss them and be saddened by their absence, and my hurt was a symbol that I, too, had lost someone who made a difference in my life. And although I lost them to a circumstance that I didn't understand, I understood that life was complicated and that I was grateful to have shared a moment of their short time here on earth.

In every circumstance we are faced with a choice. The choice to stay exactly where we are and a victim to the cards we have been dealt, or to let go, learn and grow from the situation. I wish I could say that I was brave enough to take the lesson and move forward, but I didn't. I chose to stay stuck in a cycle of poor decisions, free from feelings, free from pain.

CHAPTER 5

FINDING STRENGTH

'What if you could look ahead into your life and see what lies ahead for you? What if you could see everything you will accomplish, the success you become and the obstacles you will face to get there? What if the journey to success was nothing like you planned for – would you still go for the ride?'

–Lorenzo DeCampos (Director/Producer of *You and Me*) quoted from our film, *You and Me*

BARNEY

These are the questions that have flooded my mind for the past nineteen years, since a single moment when my life changed forever. I have experienced some of the best days and the worst days, but every single moment has been totally worth it because it has all led me to here.

After I finally graduated from high school I enrolled in a Diploma of Hospitality Management at Coffs Harbour TAFE. I had decided on this as a way for me to work flexible hours, mainly nights, and then I could surf during the day and concentrate on competitive surfing. I was fortunate that both my parents were supportive in this path that I had chosen and were excited for me when I managed to pick up a few sponsors for surfboards and clothing. To afford to travel and compete I worked at Sizzler waiting tables and as a kitchenhand. The first taste of what my life could be came in January 1998 when I was selected to compete in the Coca-Cola Junior Surf Classic; the winner would be given a wild-card entry to face Kelly Slater in the first heat of the Coca-Cola Classic, which at the time was a World Tour event. If all went to plan, this would be my epic ASP debut. In the few days leading up to the event I had been staying with my dad out at Castle Hill. He was driving me to Narrabeen every day, which was a pretty lengthy trip. After talking to the contest director Mark Warren, he invited me to stay with his family at his home so I could get some practice surfing in and save my dad the trip every day. Mark was one of Australia's surfing pioneers, so I felt extremely lucky to spend that time with him. Mark was also the contest director of the Ocean and Earth World Pro Juniors, which crowns the World Junior Champion. He invited me along to watch and introduced me to some of the top junior surfers in the world. It was so inspiring to be surrounded by the world's best and it was the motivation I needed for the coming days of competition.

On the first day of the contest I woke up early to check the waves. I was staying at the North Curl Curl Surf Club with a few other competitors: Phil and Ant MacDonald, Tom Whittaker and Darren O'Rafferty. There was a fun peaky little wave out front, which made for good competition. I made my first few heats but didn't end up with the result I was hoping for. I was stoked, though, that I had the opportunity to give it a crack in the big leagues and that Phil Macca took home the trophy. He deserved to be there and definitely gave the top dogs a run for their money. In fact, he and the other boys – aside from Ant, because he got injured – went on to qualify for the Pro Tour. Hanging with those boys over the duration of the contest showed me the standard that was expected. It gave me a whole new outlook on my approach, style and tactics for future events. I then went on to compete in regional zone and state contests, gaining good momentum but never quite reaching the potential I knew I had inside me.

Moving on from Sizzler, I got a new job as a whitewater rafting river guide at Rapid Rafting. After an intense training and qualification course I was excited to start my first day; back then I couldn't have known that this decision would change everything. A typical shift would start at the main office at the Coffs Harbour jetty around 7am. We would fill the vans with petrol and stock up with food supplies then take that day's adventure seekers out to the take-off zone, which was located ninety minutes inland on either the Goolang Creek or Nymboida River. I had never been whitewater rafting before I got the job but I quickly fell in love with it. I felt extremely lucky that I got to call this work. It was a great way to meet interesting people from all over the world, and every day was just as awesome as the previous.

Between surfing, AFL and rafting I was in the best shape ever. I was in the final year of my hospitality diploma, working with great friends and having the time of my life. I was making decent money whitewater rafting and had been saving up so I could travel and compete full-time in surfing the following year.

* * *

The day my life changed forever is in some ways crystal clear in my mind – images that have replayed over and over again through the years – and yet some details will forever be a blur. It was Easter 1999, and we had a big weekend planned. My mate was having his twenty-first party on Easter Sunday at his family's house. Both my sisters were home, along with all the boys from school and a few mates I played AFL with. I hadn't had a chance to really hang out with any of them since TAFE had resumed in February, and nothing was going to stop me from having a good time with everyone.

After Friday night out laughing and watching the Bondi Cigars play at the Sawty RSL, I woke up early on the Saturday morning to the idea of a morning at work and the sound of heavy rain. The weather was miserable but on the flip side it made for a fun day on the river. When I arrived at the office I saw we were expecting a busload of twenty clients and were down two seats, so a co-worker offered to take his van, a white early 1980s Toyota LiteAce. We loaded up the van with the day's food supply and I jumped into the passenger seat as we began the trip out west along Coramba Road to meet the busload of clients.

Despite replaying these moments again and again in my mind for quite a few years, some of the specifics – such as the songs playing on the radio, and the topic of conversation – are a bit of a blur (but it was probably something like Offspring or Blink 182). We were coming into a little town called Braunstone, the road was extremely wet and the rain was pouring down. On a two-lane road, my co-worker sped up to overtake the car ahead. I sat quietly watching as the speedometer crept up and up. The speed limit is 80 kilometres per hour and that would be on a dry sunny day; on a day like that, you wouldn't want to go any more than 60 and definitely not speed up to overtake anyone. He then proceeded to overtake a second car, and that was when I started to realise that he wasn't going to slow down. He was climbing past 120 kilometres per hour as he began to overtake a third vehicle up ahead. He showed no intention of slowing down even as he veered back into the left lane, still committed to his high speed of 130 kilometres per hour. Panic began to build as I realised we weren't going to make it, but it was too late, he hit a ninety-degree bend – and the split-second the car lost control, my memory goes blank.

You know those life-changing moments when you ponder a lot of would-have, could-have, should-have scenarios? I did at one time find myself in this headspace. Why didn't I just speak up and tell him to slow the fuck down? Why didn't I grab the wheel? But the truth is, I didn't say or do anything. It was almost as if I had an out-of-body experience where I didn't really process what was happening until it was too late, and there wasn't much I could have done to change the outcome anyway. So, once I came to terms with that, I decided to just focus on how to move forward. But forward had a very new meaning for me. Forward felt very backwards and it was heartbreaking.

From the reports, I was told that when we hit the bend in the road, the van skidded and then rolled multiple times, ejecting the driver through the window (he sustained minor injuries) while the van continued to roll before slamming into a tree. The van was crushed to half its size, with me trapped in the passenger seat in my seatbelt. My head was between my legs, and from what I have been told – I have no recollection – I was still conscious, and remained conscious the entire time it took to cut me out of the wreckage with the jaws-of-life. The cars we had overtaken were among the first on the scene. One of the drivers was a nurse, and she stayed with me until I was taken by the ambulance to Grafton Hospital. On my arrival at Grafton my family was notified and I was taken in for scans and tests.

The results indicated spinal damage and so I was prepped for the Westpac helicopter to fly me to Sydney's Royal North Shore Hospital. It was there I would be further assessed and monitored by Australia's leading spinal-injury specialists and where I would receive my official diagnosis.

I have been told my breathing and vitals were okay until I boarded the helicopter for Sydney, but then we all learnt the hard way that I am allergic to penicillin. After being given a dose to help control infection, my lungs began to shut down. Through the flight I was on oxygen, and when we landed, a team was on standby waiting for my arrival. At some stage, though, something went wrong and I started to slip away. When they removed my breathing mask to transfer me, I was dead. Thankfully they were able to resuscitate me, but I was put into an induced coma to help reduce the risk of brain damage and to allow me to rest while the initial swelling reduced. I had some pretty vivid, wild dreams that were mixed with reality.

Dream: The tube in my mouth and throat was chewing gum that I couldn't get rid of, hence I had to bite down on it constantly.

Reality: I had a tube down my throat to help me breathe, but whenever I bit down on it, alarms would be set off, so a tracheotomy – to insert an oxygen tube – was done directly into my throat.

Dream: I woke up in a room full of teddies and my head covered in bolts. As I opened the door and took a look around,

I noticed a bar at the front. I went to go and sit at the bar and hit my head on the corner of it, ripping a bolt out.

Reality: To reset my neck and spinal vertebrae, I had bolts screwed into each side of my head with a metal plate attached to a 3.5-kilogram bag of water that kept my neck aligned and stabilised. Somehow one of the screws came out and I still have a scar there today.

Among the crazy dreams, the Webbers came to visit me but it was another big morphine blur. I was sitting in the middle back seat of a bus and as each one entered the room they came from the right, walked across in front, talked to me and then walked out to the left. The most distinct thing I remember is Toby breaking down, then running out. I'd never seen or heard Toby like this. I tried to yell, 'It'll be all good, I'll be fine!' but nothing came out of my mouth.

I was in and out of consciousness for a few days but finally woke a week later with my family by my side. I was still pretty out of it though. One of my first clear memories was receiving a phone call from my sisters, Lara and Tania, and my mate Marto: they were on their way to a fundraiser that the Sawtell Saints AFL Club was hosting for me. I could hear them but because of the tracheotomy they could only just make out the words I was whispering back.

It hadn't quite clicked why they were having a fundraiser for me, but as I woke my mind was flooded with confusion about where I was and why I was there. Was I still dreaming? I looked at the male nurse who had entered my room to hold the phone for me, and then at the beeping machines surrounding my bed. I went to talk, but a sharp pain in my throat held me back. Why couldn't I talk properly? Why couldn't I move my body? Scared and increasingly confused, I managed to signal to my nurse to tell me what was happening to me.

He explained that I had broken my neck and sustained a spinal injury. I had been diagnosed a complete C6 quadriplegic, complete meaning complete paralysis with no ability to ever regain movement or function below the level of injury.

Paralysis? Quadriplegic? 'What the fuck! But I'm a surfer and a footballer. When do I get to do those things again?'

His reply held no sign of emotion, as if he had become so accustomed to these conversations. It felt like compassion had been completely sucked out of him. 'You won't be doing any of those things again. You have a ventilator to help you breathe, which you will most likely stay on forever; your right arm shows no signs of ever regaining its function. With your level of injury you won't be able to move from below the chest down to your toes or use your hands, triceps, bladder or bowels.'

Again I repeated, 'What the *fuck*! Who are you to tell me what I can or cannot do?'

'The quicker you can accept your new situation, the quicker you can learn to adapt and get on with your life,' he said with no emotion.

I then told him to get the fuck out, but because of my trachea it wasn't quite the dramatic effect I was looking for, though I'm pretty sure he could tell by my face and reading my lips that he was no longer welcome in the room.

Who was he . . . No, who was *anyone* to limit another person with their beliefs or opinions? I was fuming, I had never known anger or pain quite like this before but it lit a flame, a need and a desire to fight. This was the first time I had really been challenged in a mind–body way. Statistically the odds were stacked high against me, but deep down in my heart I knew if there was a way, I would find it. Even if I spent my whole life searching for it.

* * *

When my mum walked through the curtain, I had a sudden feeling of relief, but before I could process anything tears began to pour down my cheeks. An overwhelming sadness spread through me as she held me and we mourned the life we once knew.

I won't lie: the first few weeks were rough, for me and for everyone who cared about me. On top of my general injuries and getting my head around the idea of my life changing forever and struggling to communicate because of the tracheal tube in my throat, I caught pneumonia, and because my spinal injury had weakened my lungs, I couldn't cough. The nurses had to suction my lungs every forty-five minutes to help break up the phlegm, and then the physios would beat my chest and back to loosen as much as they could before sticking a tube down my trachea all the way to my lungs to clear it out. It felt like a razor blade scratching its way down; it was excruciating but worth the short spate of relief I would gain after.

To add to the strain, the tracheal tube meant I couldn't eat, so for the first two weeks I was fed through the tube in my throat. After the nurses were confident that I could swallow properly, I learnt to eat mashed food – basic things such as chicken or beef with peas and carrots. It wasn't at all appetising, but by that stage I was starving and anything was an upgrade from the tube food.

I had been struggling to communicate since I had woken up, so my family got creative. They made a board with the letters of the alphabet, and they would move a finger along the board till I blinked when to stop on each letter to spell out what I was trying to say. It took a lot of patience but lucky for my family they were really good at it and quick at translating for when other family and friends visited.

There were so many new feelings and lack of feeling to adjust to. Being on the ventilator was painful. It would scratch at my throat and I always felt thirsty and dry. Not being able to move my body like I used to is still something I struggle with every day. It's frustrating, it's disheartening and in the beginning it was scary. I could no longer roll around in my bed to get comfy, feel if my feet were hot or cold or even sit up. My body felt like it was numb with pins and needles in some places while in others nothing. As if it was not even part of my body anymore. It's the little things I had taken for granted like getting up to get a drink of water, standing up to pee, feeling the sand between my toes. Those were the hardest things to let go of, but also the ideals that kept me going in hopes of one day doing it all again.

One of the things that got me through those early weeks was the planning of an outing from the hospital. One of the old boys from the Sawtell Saints back home called to let me know that he and a few of the boys had put in to purchase an AFL package at the fundraiser they'd held for me a few weeks earlier. It was five VIP tickets to the Members Lounge to watch the Sydney Swans play the Collingwood Magpies at the Sydney Cricket Ground. He knew I loved the Swans and he wanted to take me as one of his guests along with a few of my mates. I had never been to a professional AFL game, and of course I wanted to go and was filled with so much excitement; but then suddenly fear struck me. How would we do it? I had never gone out, I had barely left my bed, I didn't even have a chair yet. Then the biggest question of all: How do I go with a ventilator? I didn't want to put the burden of worry on my friends, so I set myself my first goal. I had six weeks till the game and I was going to learn to breathe by myself and ditch the ventilator for good. Time was one thing I had plenty of, so from that moment I spent every waking hour working on it. The nurses were a little reluctant at first and didn't believe it was a good idea, or even possible, but I just put their opinions aside and focused on the end goal. A night of semi normality, away from nurses and tests. A night with the boys.

CHAPTER 6

THE BOTTOM OF A BOTTLE

KADA

I have spent a lot of time reflecting on this chapter and the defining moments that have led me to the place I am today, to the person I am today. I spent the longest time running away and hiding from those years, drowning in a sea of regret. It wasn't till recently that I have come to be grateful for my mistakes and own them as some of the most powerful lessons that I have ever learnt. I am honestly proud of how far I have come in the past ten years and how much I have grown as a person and discovered about myself and what this time, though difficult to live through, actually meant for me.

You know that story of Adam and Eve and the forbidden fruit? Well, in my story I am Eve and the world was my forbidden fruit. I don't know if it was just simply rebellious teenage motives or the fact that anything made out to be forbidden or wrong is twenty times more appealing. My upbringing was very strict. If you had asked me back then I would have told you I felt like I was suffocating and I missed out on a lot; today I would still agree it was rough at times, but through it all I learnt resilience.

My teenage years were tough. Like most teens my age I never quite knew my place or what I wanted, probably because I never felt I had the space or opportunity to find out. We are often conditioned by our parents and teachers to believe that someone else – someone older, with more life experience – knows best who we are, how we should act or the person we should become. In some areas of my life I was very confident, but when it came to self-belief and self-esteem in the things most dearest to me I was really lacking. I often over-compensated by trying too hard to please people even at the expense of my own values or happiness. The more I sacrificed my own needs, the more my true essence slipped away. I began to pile on mask on top of mask, a different one for each persona I created. One for my family and church, one for my school friends, one for the teachers and one for the boys. I feel exhausted just writing this, so I have no idea how I kept it up for so long. I had become convinced that this was the only way to get through the next few years, that no-one would like the real me.

I was forever chasing a particular feeling, a rush of excitement, liberation even, but I began searching in all the wrong places. I got my rush from a bottle (or the under-age classic: a box of Fruity Lexia) and I found my liberation through boys. They were at the top of the forbidden fruits yet they were the things I craved the most.

When I first started drinking with my friends, it was innocent fun. We were able to let go of all the teenage drama and just be happy to be alive. That was the feeling I quickly became addicted to and I wanted to feel like that every day. But I soon found that I needed to drink to have fun and be happy. The problem with this was that when I sobered up, I became miserable. Unbearably miserable. Major highs and then mega lows.

My friends started to catch on to my addiction and tried to sit me down for the talk. I was so deep in it, though, that I couldn't understand their concerns because all I wanted and all I needed was to fill the gaping hole of emptiness I felt inside, and the only way I knew how was to escape into a drunken haze. At the time I didn't know that these feelings were totally normal and natural; because of a few members of my church, I felt extremely judged. So, I surrounded myself with people who wouldn't question my decisions. I initially would sneak around hiding my habits from my parents but in a small town there are no secrets. I eventually gave up on being scared of the consequences and would switch off my phone, enjoy my night then deal with the backlash either when I got home or the next morning.

I was insecure, I was lost, I was a mess. Add in the drama of boys and you have yourself a recipe for disaster.

After a string of failed relationships – with one in particular taking away the last piece of self that I had, my sacred virginity, which for a young Christian girl out of wedlock is the ultimate sin – I totally switched off from feelings and consequence and said goodbye to my past of living for everyone else and decided to live for me. I had found liberation in sex and I was finally able to express myself in a way that felt truly authentic. I didn't care what it meant or what others thought, I simply went with how it made me feel.

According to my upbringing and social standards, though, I had created quite an unappealing reputation. I was called every name you could possibly think of and I was not the most popular among the girls in town. Honestly, though, I couldn't have cared less.

Men are praised for sleeping with multiple girls a night yet a woman who has multiple sex partners over a year is shunned. It was this double standard that eventually pushed me to rock bottom. I was made to feel ashamed for my actions and to believe that I truly was the names I had been called. Every day brought a new rumour about me, most untrue or manipulated, but in the eyes and ears of a small town the truth isn't what really matters. It's gossip.

It was the June long weekend and my parents had gone away for a work conference and my siblings went to my nanno and grandad's. I was supposed to stay at my friend's place but we went with a few other friends out to Wyangala Dam, which is a half-hour drive from Cowra. We met up with a group of boys from a neighbouring town, one of whom I had been seeing for a few weeks. After a few hours of drinking games, my friends were getting ready to leave. I remember opening up to my best friend, the one person I thought I could trust, about everything I had been feeling over the previous few years, the pressure to fit in and be liked and wanting to be more than what I was. I had never really shared my feelings like that before, but she reassured me that she would always be there for me. It was because of her that I found my love of journalling. She taught me to channel all my thoughts, pains and dreams into writing which then eventually became songwriting. We had a special bond that I never thought could be broken, but I guess I underestimated the lengths I would go to hide the truth.

If I could change one moment in my life, this would have been it.

I chose to spend the night with the guy I was seeing and his friends in the cabin. I said my goodbyes to the girls, assuring them that I would be fine. I didn't realise that over an hour passed as I stood outside talking with the girls before they left, and by the time I went back inside, my date had passed out. I got myself a glass of water, already starting to regret my decision to stay. His friends were still raging but suddenly I was no longer in the mood. I hopped into a vacant top bunk, thinking that the quicker I could fall asleep the sooner it would be morning. I was just dozing off when I was woken by one of the boys entering the room. He climbed up onto the bed and sat on the end. I told him to go away, that I was trying to sleep, but he kept insisting he needed to talk to me about my best friend. The thing was, I knew that she really liked him, so I decided to listen. Instead, listening actually meant him making a move. After me telling him to get off me multiple times, it suddenly hit me: he wasn't going to stop. I tried to wriggle my way out but his drunken grip was too strong. He kept telling me to 'scream louder', as if he got off on my fear and repulsion. He told me it didn't matter anyway, that everyone had passed out, so we may as well enjoy it. With tears streaming down my face, I let go. I gave in and let him have his way with me, crying the entire time. It was as if in that moment, time stopped. I feared that if I didn't give in, I had nowhere to go, nowhere to run. I was in the middle of nowhere camping with three boys I barely knew.

Later, I couldn't stop the negative thoughts and self-recrimination. How could I be so reckless? So careless? If there were ever a moment in time that I felt completely powerless, it was that night. I was so ashamed that I lied to my best friend, telling her that I simply just slept with him, because I couldn't bear the idea of saying aloud that I was held down against my will and stripped of all dignity by the boy she was obsessed with. I couldn't tell her that the guy I thought would keep me safe had passed out but then later woke and was sitting at the door as I ran out of the room. He had heard, but just sat there instead of coming in to help me. I blamed myself for years, and convinced myself that it was my own fault for putting myself in that situation, and that even if I did tell anyone they wouldn't believe me anyway due to my 'reputation'.

As I take myself back, I am reminded of the lowest moment of my life. I was consumed with so much anger and emptiness. I felt like an object, no longer a person with feelings. I was constantly reminded of what had happened by the whispers around town of why I no longer had a best friend. Knowing what I do about myself and life now, it seems ridiculous that I was ashamed to tell her the truth, but I didn't want to be a victim, I didn't want people looking at me like I was damaged goods. For so long I had been a player in everyone else's game that I wanted to be the one with all the power. So, I created the lie that I told myself for years. That it was just another night like any other.

I have many times thought about this moment but often in a place of regret and shame. I never really allowed myself to dwell in the emotions for too long because it was often too confronting. With help and guidance from a friend and mentor she helped me open my eyes to the reality of it all. That I was in fact assaulted and although I made a poor choice to stay that night, what happened next was not my fault. Knowing that I wasn't alone in this and that I am not the only one who has dealt with this kind of sexual assault has given me the courage to share this with you now. My story is one of many and I just wish I had been more educated on the power of self-love sooner. It is with self-love that we can learn to heal and grow stronger from every experience we encounter. We are brave enough to know our worth and fight for it.

Unfortunately it took quite a few years for me to come to learn this valuable life lesson, and things began to spiral downward pretty quickly after that night.

* * *

They say things happen in threes. My wake-up call came to me in three stages. I had become dependent on alcohol to get through the night, to ward off the same vivid nightmare replaying over and over, each time seeing a different scenario in which I may have been able to escape. These were the types of vicious thoughts that haunted me for a long time and the reason I didn't want to think or feel. But after a while the alcohol started to affect my health. One night, when I was fifteen, it landed me in hospital with excruciating stabbing pains in my pelvis. I was transferred to Orange District Hospital, which was located about an hour's drive away, with suspected appendicitis. This was probably my first shake-up. I was scared and terrified of the thought of surgery. I begged my parents to not let me go in, but my condition was so serious the nurses wheeled me away in my bed and prepped me for my operation.

The following morning, my parents arrived just before the doctor came to talk about the surgery. My appendix seemed to be fine, but for safety measures they removed it anyway. This seemed extremely odd to me, but luckily the human body is incredible at adapting. The results did come back, though, showing cysts on my ovaries. The pain I experienced was the cysts enlarging and bursting caused by a disease in the ovaries called endometriosis.

After the hospital ran its tests, I came to realise that the continual late booze-filled nights were flaring up the symptoms of my endometriosis. My diet was anything but healthy; KFC chips and gravy were often on the menu, which didn't help my mood swings. My Aunty Jess was one of the nurses on duty, and one afternoon she and my mum came to my room to talk. They were worried, and tried to make me see that though they understood that I was hurting, in the process I was also hurting everyone around me. I was so numb and closed off that I just stared at the ceiling in silence, but it was the first time in a long time that I didn't answer back defensively. I just listened to their pain; pain I had caused.

I agreed that I would at least try, and they signed me up to alcohol counselling at the hospital.

Sixteen years old and in alcohol counselling, my life had hit a whole new low. I had left school to start a hairdressing apprenticeship and when that didn't work out I started working at a toy store by day and a video store in the afternoons and evenings. How did I even have time to party? They say addicts are very resourceful and although that is what I had been labelled I never really identified myself as an addict. I just didn't have a purpose bigger than myself and I didn't know how to deal with life when it threw me off course.

I had no expectations for the counselling meetings, no idea that it would help, but somewhere deep down I must have wanted to try, if not for me, then for the stress I had put on my family. The doctor was nice and welcoming. She started by talking about herself to make me feel comfortable and then listened without judgement. I didn't go into much detail about my life but it felt nice to just finally say out loud why I had struggled so much with alcohol. I didn't like who I was or where I was in my life and I wanted to escape from it. She congratulated me on being brave enough to admit that, and offered suggestions and exercises to do if I found myself in a situation where I was tempted to drink.

I spent a few months working on keeping myself clean and on the straight and narrow. I even decided to go back to church with my family. But something was still missing in my heart. I still felt suffocated by the rules, and afraid that my every move was being judged. But my compliance minimised the stress in my family, so I again played along. Pretty soon, though, I found myself back to old habits. Yo-yoing between my Christian practices and my social excesses. Living a double life.

* * *

I loved the sense of security and stability I felt around the people of my church yet I never felt empowered to discover my strengths. Instead in some ways I felt powerless and ashamed of the desires I was having and again, I wanted more.

The second wake-up call came to me at 7am on Sunday, 28 January 2007. I received a phone call from a friend telling me that our mutual friend Chad had died in a drink-driving accident the previous night. My heart sank. *Not again. This can't be happening again.* We had seen him the night before and never thought it would be our last time with him. Chad was another one of those charismatic beings. His laugh changed the mood in a room instantly, and if you asked anyone who knew him their top ten stories in life, they would most likely all include Chad. How much loss can one town take? One group of friends?

As I cried I was reminded of life, its imperfections but most of all its gift. And for all of our friends we had lost, I wanted to live, for them and for me.

I had been making positive changes in my life and I wanted more. I asked my parents if they would help me move to Sydney with a girlfriend. Still not convinced this change was long-lasting, my dad sat me down and said he wouldn't help me move to Sydney because he didn't believe it was the right environment for me to be in by myself at that stage. I understood where he was coming from and truthfully, it wasn't really Sydney I wanted to move to, it was anywhere but home.

The third wake-up call came one night after I had watched a movie at a friend's place and then decided to walk home. Now looking back, I was crazy because it was a four-kilometre walk; I don't really know why I didn't ask for a lift. There's something peaceful about walking in the dark.

I was about halfway home when I heard yelling. I kept walking but the screams got louder and louder till I realised they were directed at me. I was confused by the two girls who were approaching me. I thought we were friends, but suddenly it did not appear that way as they came at me with accusations and threats, getting closer and closer. I turned and walked away from them but one grabbed my ponytail, ripping my head back, kneeing me in the back and making me drop to the ground. At first I tried to get away screaming at them to please stop, but then I had a flashback to the night in the cabin and I curled my body into a ball, closed my eyes and let them do it. I tried to protect my face as they repeatedly kicked me all over. Again, I chose not to fight back. Even though I knew they were wrong to attack me, in some ways I felt I needed this beating to knock some sense into me. To trigger all the emotions I had trapped inside. To finally wake me from my revolving cycle of bad choices.

Some say there are five stages of grief. For me, all my stages came flooding in at once. Anger, depression, denial, bargaining, acceptance, anger, anger, anger. But at least it was feeling and I was no longer numb and running away. I was finally ready to face it all head-on and let it go.

* * *

Though these were the hardest days of my life, I am grateful for every experience. With every hardship, I found strength I never knew I had. It may have taken me a few years of spiralling off the path to get back on track but with time, I have found forgiveness and gratitude for every person and experience along my journey.

CHAPTER 7

CHALLENGE ACCEPTED

BARNEY

I have set myself many goals over the past thirty-eight years of life, but my challenge to learn to breathe independently has probably been the most terrifying one I have ever made. I would be lying if I said I wasn't scared or that I never had moments of doubt, but there is something extremely satisfying and rewarding about defying the odds. Words like 'impossible' and 'no' became the fuel to my fire. Even though it terrified me, I knew this was the first step I needed to take towards my recovery. In some ways I think I was one of the lucky ones: I was surrounded by so much support and love from family and friends, and I believe it was due to a combination of this support and my goals that allowed me to move forward and never fall into a 'Why me?' depression.

I woke up ready and excited to test out my lungs. I had a whole medical team on standby. I laughed at the formality they brought to the occasion. Everything was going to be fine, I told them – I was just capping off the ventilator to let my lungs do what they were supposed to do. Breathe.

I took one last breath through the ventilator as the nurse unplugged and capped off the tube. I was ready to take in my first real breath in weeks, but something inside me freaked. I couldn't breathe in or out and I felt trapped, like I was suffocating. They must have seen the panic in my eyes and quickly reconnected me to the machine. I had lasted about three seconds. As I began to catch my breath, my eyes filled with tears and I broke down. How could my body turn on me like that? How could it not know what it is meant to do? My mum sat by my side, wiping my tears away. I know all mums have a superhero-like way of making everything feel better, but during these days my mum gave me hope. I could see the pain in her eyes as she watched me suffer, but I could also see the belief she had in me to pull through. Sometimes you need something bigger than yourself to be the reason you try. She had always said to me, 'The power to win comes from within,' and those words never rang more true. I wanted to do this for her, so it would be one less thing that she had to worry about because life was already going to be harder on her. I knew that if I could pull this off I'd have the strength to keep going, one day at a time.

I was allowed only one attempt a day at breathing independently. I replayed what went wrong over and over all afternoon and into the night. I couldn't stop thinking about my next attempt. It was a mixture of anxiety and adrenalin as I planned how I could beat the three-second score I had set for myself. Three seconds doesn't seem long, but I discovered that it can feel like an eternity. But, after knowing what to expect this time round, I gave myself a pep talk and told myself to remain calm. Basically I had to rebuild a new relationship with my body and regain its trust, and I had to learn to also trust that it would do what I needed it to do.

The following day the whole medical team gathered again by my bed ready for attempt number two. I wasn't as confident this time round and my anxiety was through the roof, but I was ready to give it another go. With my mum alongside me again, I gave the nurse the nod and she clamped off the tube. The timer started – and stopped ten seconds later as she reattached the tube to the ventilator. I did it, I beat my three-second record! To most, ten seconds might not seem long, but to me right in that moment it was an eternity of uncertainty. Was I going to take that next breath? When I did it was the best feeling to know that I had it in me to overcome this first challenge.

The next day everyone again congregated back in my room for attempt number three. Two minutes done. With every breath I took independently a new wave of hope and confidence flooded through me. Day four was a good day: I went from two minutes to forty minutes. I never knew how exhausting it could be to simply breathe. Each time, I retreated into my head, having internal conversations back and forth trying to convince myself that I could keep going, then talking myself out of it, to then reassuring myself that I was doing great. I think that actually may have been the most exhausting part of it all.

Day five took me from forty minutes to two hours and then on day six, two hours to five days. In some ways it was hard to get used to the fact that I was breathing by myself day and night while on the other hand it was the most normal thing I had been able to do for myself in weeks. The medical team came in to assess my progress during the fifth day of my independent breathing.

'Five days down,' I said extremely proud.

'Five days?' replied the nurse. 'Well, if you can make it to seven we'll remove the tracheal tube from your throat and we can start the conversation about transferring you out of intensive care to the spinal unit.'

So, I had to make another two days. Forty-eight hours doesn't seem long, but it would be the most stressful two days of my life. What if I didn't make it? Would that mean I had to start again? I really wanted to get out of ICU and go upstairs to the spinal unit but I kept second-guessing myself. I even came to a point where I freaked myself out so much I almost gave up – but right at the last second a voice inside reassured me that I could do it.

Even though I was lying flat all day, learning to breathe normally really took it out of me. For my attempt at seven days, I spent the first five simply focusing on my breath but during the final two days I was able to relax into it a little more. As I learnt to let go and let it be, I had more time to think about the whole situation. How different my life had become and was going to be. Only a few weeks earlier I was so independent and ready for the world, now I could barely breathe by myself, I couldn't shower or dress myself. Even my bladder and bowel had lost their independence. I had in my head that if I could prove them all wrong with learning to breathe, then maybe they were wrong about it all. Because how could I possibly live without walking, running, surfing?

* * *

It was a month to the day after my accident, and a bed was available in the spinal unit. I had made it to the seven days of breathing independently, and so the medical staff came in with a couple of wardsmen to help move me.

'But I still have the tracheal tube in my neck,' I said.

'We'll sort that out upstairs,' the nurse replied.

I had not left the room since I'd arrived, so I was excited for a change of scenery. I still couldn't sit up, because I was having issues with stabilising my blood pressure and I had been lying down for four weeks straight. Any slight movement upwards made me feel lightheaded to the point where I would pass out. I was beginning to learn that nothing was going to be straightforward or an easy transition – at least for a while. It was going to be a lot of hard work and perseverance, but I was determined to stick it out.

I arrived in my new room, which I was to share with three other patients. I was allocated Bed 07. The nurses came in shortly after I arrived to remove the tracheal tube from my throat. For the past week, I had dreamt of this moment and now that the time had arrived, I was filled with butterflies. Would it hurt? How would the gaping hole in my neck close up? There I was again, turning myself in mental circles, so instead I closed my eyes and braced for pain – and just like that, it was out. It definitely did hurt but it was also an instant relief, like an annoying itch in my throat had finally been scratched properly. They covered the hole with a big bandaid and told me I could now speak. I mouthed a soft *thank you*, in the same way I had been speaking since I woke up, and the nurse laughed. 'No, silly, you can really talk now.' And then I found my voice. 'Oh, thank you.'

Wow. That day already felt like a very successful one. I was no longer dependent on a machine to breathe for me and I could finally communicate. It's probably a good thing I couldn't talk out loud when I first heard my prognosis, because you can imagine the words that would have echoed throughout the hospital.

That afternoon I was given permission to go downstairs – in my bed – into the courtyard to see the sun. There's something about the warmth and feeling that the sun has on the body: it was an instant mood elevator and soon became a daily ritual. The fresh air – especially when I breathed into my lungs unassisted – the sun and greenery was a much better view than the bleak walls and stale air-conditioner recirculating all the sickness inside the hospital.

That first day in the spinal unit I was still unable to move my arms much, but I was given a buzzer left by my side to alert the nurses if I needed anything throughout the day or night. This was my first night without the safety of the ventilator or the immediate attention from hospital staff. It was a stepping stone towards finding more independence within my injury. I was kept awake a lot of the night by the snoring of other patients and I guess a bit of anxiety about being in a new place with all new people. There is a lesser level of care in the spinal unit than the ICU, which I was made aware of in the transition. I had a brief moment where I panicked at the thought that I might not be able to reach the buzzer all night if I needed something, but I managed to breathe myself through it and eventually fell asleep.

I woke the following morning tired but also relieved to have made it through the night without any major problems. That day was my first day of physio and ability assessments. It had been a month since the accident, so they were able to get a clearer indication of how my spinal injury had affected the function of my body. A nurse arrived with a reclining wheelchair for me to be transferred to the gym, where I met my physio team. I was given hand splints to wear anytime I was just lying around, and

I tried doing hand weights. It sounds simple, but it totally wiped me. I had constant dizzy spells, unable to sustain the energy to get through the session. This showed me that if I was to progress and prove myself to the specialists, first I needed to get used to being upright, and fast. Every time I sat upright, though, I passed out. It was a gradual process of being positioned upright, passing out, being laid flat with my legs raised above heart level to regain consciousness, and then trying all over again.

This was a great lesson in learning to listen to my body. My ego would tell me to stop complaining, to push through and get it done, whereas my body would say, *one step at a time*. The mind games were exhausting, but I knew that no-one else could do it for me. This was my battle.

Every time I had a positive gain, though, it felt counterbalanced by something negative. I had a hard time regulating my temperature after every shower, so I would lie shivering under four blankets for hours until it was time for my PT (physical therapy) and OT (occupational therapy) sessions. It was a frustrating cycle; the athlete in me was always craving more but my body just wasn't ready yet. I was soon to learn that patience was key.

It was comforting to have my dad close by. He and his wife, Sue, visited me regularly as they lived in Sydney. We often watched the car races and talked about sports and life. He would always give me good advice if I ever felt down.

After a few weeks, I had finally started to regain strength, and I was managing to be upright in a chair more regularly. The AFL game that I had been working so hard to attend with the boys was fast approaching. Having that goal had kept me motivated through the previous month and I was so excited to go out for the first time. Everyone in the hospital was nice and took good care of me, but what I was really looking forward to was being treated as a normal man, and not coddled. My mum, on the other hand – well, she was terrified at the thought but also understood that for my own sanity I needed this.

You would never think it, but one of my favourite memories was created during this time, when my mum's partner, Malcolm, came to visit me. I hadn't had a proper chance to talk to Malcolm or thank him for being there for Mum through all of this, and I was so grateful to have him in our lives. I remember him being a bit nervous talking to me, but then he finally said it: he wanted to know if he could have my blessing to marry my mum. This was one of those really special moments in which, no matter how hard life had been, I couldn't help but feel pure happiness for them both, especially Mum. She had been through so much pain and sadness, and she deserved this happiness. I was honoured to have him officially become my step-dad.

* * *

It was the night before the game, and just when I thought it was finally smooth sailing from there, another curveball. This one, by the name of Autonomic Dysreflexia. This medical condition occurs in a person with a spinal-cord injury when they have a trauma below the level of their injury. It is a signal that something is wrong in the form of extremely high blood pressure, which if left untreated can be fatal. It is most commonly triggered by a blocked catheter, broken bones or blocked bowels. My family and I had been trained by the medical staff in the spinal ward on what to do in this situation but had not experienced an episode until now. My trigger was a blocked catheter. It all started with a rash that looked like an allergic reaction, and an excruciating pounding thud behind my eyes. It felt as though my head could explode off my shoulders at any moment. I was given some blood-pressure medication in a pump spray under the tongue that helped lower it almost immediately, and after they flushed my catheter they changed it for a new one. It all happened so quickly and efficiently but was only just caught in time.

These traumatic events brought on new waves of worry for my mum. She didn't want to let me go to the game, but after the boys were all drilled on what to do and confirmed over and over that I was carrying a medical card that stated what to do in the case of an emergency, her worry eased. I was determined that nothing was going to bring down this day that I had been looking forward to for weeks.

The boys arrived and I was in my chair ready to go at 10am. We had been rushing to be ready in time, and I hadn't given myself enough time to adjust to being seated upright. I was overwhelmed and quickly becoming faint. As they were wheeling me downstairs I began to feel shaky and blacked out. My mum was almost too eager to pull the pin and take me back upstairs, but as soon as she even started the question – Did I still . . . – I interrupted her with, 'I'll be okay, Mum, I just need a second.'

I think the excitement and adrenalin were getting to me. Finally we were doing this, I was going out for the day and I was going to have fun with the boys. The nurse gave me an injection to help control my nausea, and off we went. My mate Grohl pushed me into the wheelchair-accessible cab and the driver strapped me in. I smiled out at my mum, who had tears streaming down her face. I'm sure they were a mixture of feelings, happy and sad. Happy that we had made it this far but sad that she had to anxiously wait for my return.

The energy at the SCG was electric. It was a sold-out game of 48 000 people, and Sydney Swans legend Tony Lockett kicked his 1300th goal, so it was an exciting event to be part of. I was pretty pumped to crack open my first beer in months, but when we said our cheers and I took in the first sip, something was different. This had been the longest I had gone without a drink for years, so I was expecting a refreshing experience. That wasn't the case, though. It didn't agree with me, and I barely got through a few sips. I was disappointed but also determined to have a good time, so I just let it go and set myself a new goal: to be able to finish a beer. The game ended with the Swans coming out on top. It was an amazing day and a memory I am so grateful for. It was exactly what I needed in that moment: a reminder that friendship is the best medicine and I had some of the best quality ones in the world.

When we arrived back at the ward I was physically exhausted, so I went straight to bed but the rush of the day kept me wide awake. Before my mum left for the night, she hugged me and said, 'My darling, if your first outing can be in a crowd of 48 000 people, then you can cope with anything.'

CHAPTER 8

FINDING KATE

KADA

For the Easter holidays of 2007 I decided to visit Coffs Harbour to see my cousin Gabby and some family friends. Though I was only going for two weeks I cried when I said goodbye to my parents, as if I knew I wouldn't be home with them for much longer.

It had been quite a few years since I had been to Coffs and I had forgotten how much I loved it. The minute I arrived, I felt at peace and excited for the future. I don't know if it was the ocean air or the beach itself but I knew that this was where I belonged. I called my mum every day, begging her to send my things up and let me stay but every

day the answer was: *No, you can't run away, it will all be fine.*
Every day I persisted, and I could hear in her voice that she
knew deep down that she would eventually lose me to this
beautiful place.

Gabby had to work most days, so I spent pretty much all
of my time exploring the beaches and wandering through
the shops. My heart melted, though, the first time I spent the
day in Sawtell. It had a charm that simply felt right. I hadn't
experienced this kind of happiness since I was a kid. I was in
a place where nobody knew my past and I could rewrite my
story. I had some close family friends from the area whom I
had known since I was young. Twins Michael and Richard had
been kind enough to show me around. Living ten hours
away meant they had been sheltered from my cocktail of
bad choices but it didn't stop them from knowing that I had
been having a hard time. I was always closest to Richard;
he made me feel safe and he brought out the good in me.
I wanted to be the person that he saw. There was a time I
thought maybe we would one day end up together because
he was what I needed in my life: stability, plus he made me
really happy. I know a lot of people thought the same, but
even though on paper we were the perfect fit, to both of us
we were nothing more than great friends, which is really
exactly what I needed. Their friendship got me through a lot
and reminded me that the young vibrantly happy girl they
grew up with was still inside me.

After my Easter visit I was sad to say goodbye but somehow I knew it wouldn't be for long. I went home with a new lease on life. I was ready for change and ready to be more than what I had been.

Things went really well for a few weeks, but soon enough the small-town drama reignited and before I knew it I was back into the same old bad habits of partying and taking comfort in the wrong types of boys.

I knew something had to change, but like all things that we know are good for us, I made excuses for why I couldn't stop. Why I kept going back to the same parties and why every night would end in the same intoxicating mess. It was like I felt I had something to prove to everyone. I had created this party-girl reputation and I soon discovered that the bolder my choices, the more buzz I would create. I got a real kick out of knowing that whatever I had done would cause a chain reaction and the whispers would spread like wildfire around the town. When my friends would come to me worried with the news of the latest story being spread about me, I would often laugh it off, telling them that none of this would matter when I moved to America for my music career. I always hid that comment behind a joke, though, scared of what people might say if they knew I was serious about it. I imagined their comments – 'She must think she's sooo good,' and 'What makes her think she has what it takes?' – which were actually the questions I was throwing at myself every day.

I think the truth was I wanted to matter. I wanted to have a purpose and I wanted people to care about what I was doing with my life. I didn't want to be a follower and hide in the shadows where no-one remembered me, I wanted to live outside the box of normal and create my own path. I never did like rules but I just looked for attention and recognition in all the wrong ways.

Sometimes I would lock myself in my room and listen to loud music and dance in my underwear, or I would sit at my piano and write. Every time I did it, I asked myself why I didn't do this more often and promised myself to do it every day. I convinced myself though that no-one wanted to hear my journal of songs, so again I locked away a piece of myself. I kind of liked it like that, though, because I felt that if I didn't share that part of me, then no-one could take it away or try to tear it apart.

After seeing the difference in me when I came home from my holiday in Coffs Harbour, how happy I was, joining in family outings and helping my mum around the house, my poor parents could now see me slipping away again. By this stage I was the eldest of five. I was seventeen, Rachael was thirteen, Clarissa was nine, Annabelle, five and Daimon was two. I had been largely absent throughout the previous few years and missed so much of their lives. I wasn't the big sister or role model they deserved, and I didn't really know how to be. I remember Rachael so desperately wanting to hang out with me all the time, and I took it for granted. I didn't know then how honoured I should have been to be able to influence the lives of three younger sisters and a brother.

It was a Tuesday afternoon in June 2007 and my dad came home from work one day with sadness in his eyes. He sat me down and asked me if I was happy living there. My answer was no. The next few words to come out of his mouth were probably the hardest ones he had ever had to say to anyone. He said, 'I have a few days off work from Thursday. You're moving to Coffs Harbour.'

I didn't know how to process my feelings. I was so excited at the thought of leaving and starting fresh in a place that I just knew was going to be wonderful for me, but I also felt a sudden, intense sadness to know that I was leaving my family.

The next night we arranged for a family farewell dinner with my nanno, grandad, aunties, uncles and cousins. I finally felt like everything was going to be okay and things would start to get better for me. I distinctly remember my Aunty Jess and Uncle Nathan being mad at my parents for sending me away, but I could tell they were just scared. I mean, I was seventeen and moving ten hours away but I was grateful to know that I had relatives, and Michael and Richard's family close by, if I needed anything. After my family left, I went out to meet up with a few friends to say my goodbyes. It was the end of an era, but one I was happy to let go of, and the beginning of a whole new life for me.

We packed the car and one by one I turned to my family to give them one last hug and kiss. Daimon was too young to understand but I gave him a kiss and told him I loved him. Clarissa and Annabelle ran at me with their arms wide open, bawling their eyes out begging me not to go. Rachael was coming for the road trip, so she said her quick goodbyes and hopped into the ute while I stood and stared at Mum. I burst into tears, apologising and telling her how much I loved her and would miss her. I was sorry for all of the pain and worry I had caused her but now she wouldn't need to worry anymore. I was going to change. I had to. She pulled me in tight, wiping away my tears and telling me that she had and always would love me and would always be there for me no matter what.

The car ride was quiet. As Dad drove, I slept a lot, and when I wasn't asleep I stared out the window wondering what my new life would be like. This wasn't going to be the same as Cowra. I had new responsibilities and I was also determined to lock away that part of my life and never let it see the light of day again.

After a stopover in Tamworth with my cousins, we woke early the next morning to get back on the road. That day felt different; I was anxious and started to doubt my ability to go through with this. My dad had arranged for me to move in with a friend of Gabby's, and I started to panic about the thought of living with a complete stranger.

When we arrived at my new home, though, my excitement returned. It was a two-bedroom apartment right on the main street of Sawtell, just a walk away from the beach and the shops. I didn't have my licence yet but there was a bus stop just outside that would take me into town, but everything I could ever need was right there within walking distance. My new flatmate Rachel welcomed us with a warm hug. We took a little walk around and then jumped back in the ute to meet up with Gabby, Michael and Richard.

When we said our final goodbyes I hugged my sister Rachael and told her that she was now the big sister of the house and to be patient and kind with the others. Saying goodbye to my dad was one of the most heartbreaking things I have ever done. He held me so tight, as if he never wanted to let me go. I'm sure this was one of the hardest decisions he ever had to make but we both knew it was for the best. He also made me a promise that the rest of my family would move up to join me within a few years, so I had that to hold on to. For those last few moments of him holding me, him as my dad, me as his daughter, I cried with heartache over all the horrible things I had put them through. I wanted so badly to have my independence that I took for granted the wonderful loving family I had. I was so determined to believe that they had just wanted to punish me all the time, that I couldn't see that they were just doing the best they knew how. I should have said *thank you* more often and *I love you* every time I said goodbye. Every bad memory of the previous few years flooded through me until my dad snapped me out of it. He said, 'There is nothing you can do or say to me to make me stop loving you. You are my daughter.'

* * *

I finally had what I had wanted for so long: freedom. But as I sat taking everything in, I wondered why it didn't feel as good as I'd thought it would. You know those sayings: *Be careful what you wish for*, and *You don't know what you've got till it's gone?* They were beginning to resonate strongly.

That first night I tossed and turned as the reality of what I had done sank in. The next morning I woke early, tired but excited to start my new life.

The plan was that my parents would get me set up and support me while I settled in and looked for a job. I had a few weeks to find my feet though before I started handing out my résumé, so I wanted to make the most of my time getting to know my new home.

Rachel and I walked to the beach so she could surf, and as I watched her paddle out I couldn't help but smile at the ocean – it was just as beautiful as I had remembered it. I couldn't believe how warm the air was for winter. I was used to being totally rugged up breathing fog, but no, not in Sawtell; it was cool but the sun was warm and toasty.

This was the perfect start to the day, and it soon became my morning habit: I would walk to the beach saying hi to strangers and then finish with a quick swim before running home to a nice hot shower. I had never had a ritual like this before and it felt great.

Rachel was a clean eater and very environmentally conscious. I didn't even know what that meant – I knew how to recycle, but I had never thought about the environment as a living thing that needed to be cared for – and she definitely opened my eyes to a new way of living.

After a few weeks of watching Rachel and everyone else surf, I wanted to try. Rachel lent me her Mini Mal and gave me a couple of tips, but I stupidly told her that I had surfed before – by which I meant I had bodyboarded, the kind you do in between the flags – so I was left to fend for myself out there. It was an overcast, windy day, so I decided I would just hang in the whitewash, all the time wondering how everyone else made it look so easy. I couldn't even control the board enough to face the right direction, let alone catch anything. Just as I decided to give up and go back in to shore I managed to turn around to catch the whitewash in. Obviously I wasn't in the right position on the board, though, because I nose-dived and it flew up and hit me, splitting my eyebrow open. I really should have just taken a lesson. I headed back to our apartment feeling a bit defeated but determined that I would fit in here.

Even though I already had some friends in Sawtell, I wanted to make new ones who knew nothing about my past. After all, it was a new place and a new me. So, one day when I was shopping in one of the boutiques in town I got chatting to the owner, and when she told me her name was Fiona, I replied, 'Hi, I'm Kate.' Wait, *what*? I had always been Kathryn. Where had this come from? Well, a girl I knew was also named Kathryn but had always been called Kate. I had always thought it was cool, so on a sunny afternoon in a boutique in Sawtell, I became Kate Southwell. It felt good, I felt my past melt away and for the first time in a long time, I was excited to be me.

CHAPTER 9

IT'S ADAPTING NOT ACCEPTING

BARNEY

After a month in the spinal unit I made the move to Moorong, the Spinal Injury Unit at the Royal Rehabilitation Centre in Ryde. There, I would learn how to adapt to my new life as a quadriplegic in a wheelchair.

I remember crying to my mum the night before I moved. I was nervous about the transition, scared that this was it, the last phase and last chance to prove the medical experts wrong about the kind of life I was capable of leading. I wasn't sure if I was ready. I didn't want to hear them tell me all the things I couldn't do, despite the statistics. Because statistically speaking, with my level of injury as a complete C6 quadriplegic, there was no possible way to regain movement below my chest down to the lower limbs and in the triceps, abs and hands. 'They will never recover.' It's words like these that kill any chance of hope and that subconsciously stick with a person forever. But the statistics had also told me I would be on a ventilator forever. I just needed to cling to that and remain focused.

I was a public patient, so again I was to share a room with three others. It was crazy to hear the stories of how everyone else had ended up there. Motorbike and car accidents weren't as common as I would have thought, but I heard tales of surgeries gone wrong and police shoot-outs. I was also surprised to hear how many had so quickly accepted their prognosis and were ready to move on with their new life. I was nowhere near there yet.

It was such a relief to be out of hospital and in a new environment. There were so many nice places to sit and hang out in the sun outdoors. It was kind of like camp. There was a games room, a dining hall, kitchen and a huge rehab gym containing a lot of new fancy equipment that I couldn't wait to use: standing frames, motorised cycle machines and a hydrotherapy pool. I had missed being in the water and even though it wasn't the ocean, it was still water and where I felt most alive, and I couldn't wait to use it.

I had a few days to adjust before my program started. I met my new physio team and told them my goals of what I wanted to try, only to be shut down with their more realistic ideas about mastering transfers and completing simple tasks that were considered appropriate for my level of injury. I didn't let their lack of optimism affect my focus, though. I was there to learn as much as I could and work hard. My biggest frustration was not being able to have a one-on-one session with my therapist, because there were always multiple patients at a time, so I chose to put in extra time in the gym on weekends to connect to the motorised cycling machine. I needed to get these legs moving and keep the circulation pumping.

My mate Leigh Webber had just moved to Sydney, and he came to hang out with me most days, which made a huge difference. It was a pretty good feeling when I was able to use the standing frame. Leigh would strap me in and pump the chair up and make me dance. He would also take me out to the movies or we would go across to the pub. Every day and every outing made me feel a little more like my old self.

The previous few months had been all about the things I had lost — the ability to walk, to feed myself, to pee, to sit up, to roll over, wriggle my toes and feet, dress myself and even to shake hands — but while this was more than devastating, there was one thing I never lost: my friends. I am so thankful, and I have undoubtedly the greatest friends anyone could have. They really stepped up and showed me the true meaning of friendship, through constant phone calls, cards and visits; I don't think they could have shown me any more how much they cared. The funny thing is that no-one had mobile phones back then, so if I had a phone call it had to come through the main nurses' office and the nurse would bring me the phone. But I got so many phone calls so regularly that I often kept the main phone in my room, and if it rang I would answer, 'Moorong Spinal Unit, Nurse David speaking.' Nine times out of ten it was for me.

One afternoon I received a call from a mate Joel 'Tubby' Bath. It was always so good to hear from the boys back home and keep up to date with what was happening. He was in Year 12 doing his HSC exams and had decided for his Design and Technology Project that he was going to create a surf competition in my name, 'The Barney Miller Charity Surf Classic' and raise money to help with my medical bills. Of course he wanted me to be there. I was so pumped, and also humbled by the fact that he would want to do that for me and my family. It really spoke the truth of how amazing my mates were and still are.

The date was set and I had just over a month to work out how I could attend the competition. It was a good test to see how I would cope in the real world. First I needed to organise flights and wheelchair-accessible accommodation, because my mum's house was being renovated to not only make it accessible for me but also to fit Mal and his six kids. I also needed daily nurses who would help with my morning routine while home for the weekend. It was a bit daunting, making sure we organised everything, but also another exciting thing to keep me motivated and moving forward.

In the meantime I focused on becoming as strong as possible for my trip home. The idea of all my old friends seeing me as I was now in a wheelchair made me feel anxious, but I was determined to get there and show them how well I was doing. At the rehab centre I didn't mingle much with the other patients – most of the time I had visitors to keep me occupied – but there was one guy named Fred with whom I had struck up a friendship. He was a paraplegic who was regaining significant movement in his lower limbs. He told me about an author named Bob Proctor and his book *You Were Born Rich*. I got the audio tapes and started listening to them straightaway, but I didn't finish them. I was a twenty-year-old boy with the attention span of a child, so back then I guess I wasn't really as focused as I thought I was, but little did I know that in years to come the words of Bob Proctor would be words that I would live by every day.

* * *

After the initial excitement of getting to rehab, the days all started to roll into each other. Deep down I always felt that with the right support I could somehow train my body to work again in the long term, but unfortunately the physio team focused instead on the short-term, simpler aims. So, I kept my goals to myself, but I never gave up on them.

When I finally got to move into my own room, some of the boys came to celebrate. They would often come to visit and bring beers, and we would regularly be in trouble for being too rowdy. I needed whatever distraction I could get to make the time go by more quickly, to take my mind off my disappointed hopes of what I could achieve there. When my friends and family weren't visiting, I felt empty and alone. I hated the feeling of loneliness yet I wasn't ready to go home either. I didn't really know where I belonged. I didn't allow myself to dwell over those feelings often; usually it happened when no-one was around, which I think is why I surrounded myself with people for so many years.

My mum had tried to keep me out of the legalities surrounding the accident up until this point to allow me time to heal, but it was now time to tell my side of the story. Tom Goudkamp from Stacks Law Firm (which is now Stacks Goudkamp) came to meet me while I was still in hospital, but I wasn't ready to talk then. I told my mum I was now ready to have a meeting with the lawyer and they arranged for him to come to Moorong. We sat down in the common room and he started with simply getting to know me, who I was, my aspirations in life and what my life was at that stage. He then explained how he could help me in my case for compensation. At first, I was a little uncomfortable about the situation. I felt like I didn't need it because this wasn't going to be forever, but after an extensive conversation he made me realise the reality of my situation. It was no longer about whether or not I believed I could beat this, and I had to take into consideration how long I could be fighting for. I had to think about my mum and the fact that I was already going to be dependent on her so much and I couldn't bear the thought of being a financial burden on her too. I learnt that for someone with my injury, the average cost of living for the first year – including house modifications, transport, nursing and caring services, wheelchairs, bathroom mobility, lifting machines and medical supplies – is close to one million dollars. And that doesn't include non-traditional therapies. It's ironic that in order for me to be able to afford to even try to get better, even to go home, I had to admit defeat to the severity of my injury and accept that it is something I will live with for the rest of my life. This was something I had an incredibly tough time coming to terms with.

* * *

The day finally arrived when I was able to go home to Sawtell for the weekend for the Barney Miller Surf Classic. The cab arrived to take us to the airport and my mum and I did our last run over the checklist. Checking in and boarding went pretty smoothly. The airline staff were very helpful and accommodating to our every need. It was such a surreal feeling to be on my way home, I couldn't wipe the smile off my face. We were ready for a weekend of paradise. I was so excited to see everyone, but also my beagle, Kirra. Some mates had been looking after her for me, and I had missed her so much.

As we were flying in over Sawtell it was so nice to have those few moments to take it all in. The raw beauty of the coastline, the waves crashing onto the shore and the green mountains. This was Mother Nature's masterpiece in all its glory; I was home.

We were welcomed at the airport by all the boys and Malcolm. It was overwhelming but awesome to be back with everyone. First thing on the agenda was to head straight to Southies Headland to check the surf. It had been too long since I'd been able to just sit and watch the waves. I wanted to visualise myself on them. Everything was exactly how I remembered it but better, and I suddenly had a whole new appreciation for it all. Just to feel the ocean breeze was amazing.

After the surf check we went back to my mates' house to see Kirra. She came to greet us when we arrived and instead of running at me with a surge of excitement like she usually did, she slowly walked towards me. It was as if she sensed that something was wrong. She came close to sniff me, then the boys helped me tilt my head down towards her and she dropped and rolled over for me to scratch her belly. I had missed her so much.

After hanging out for a bit, they helped me into the car to take me to our accommodation at Pacific Bay Resort. It felt weird being home but not staying in my house or in Sawty. The hotel was on the other side of Coffs Harbour, about a twenty-minute drive, but it was wheelchair accessible and we had to be practical. The main thing was that I was home.

* * *

Later that afternoon we went to see a man who became my first mentor. He changed my life and my way of thinking. His name was Arthur Pascoe. Arthur was a grandmaster in Zen Shiatsu and he had lived what I was going through. He was a champion gymnast when, at the age of thirty, he was practising a floor routine and lost control and ended up falling down a few stairs on the side of the mat. He broke his neck and back and was paralysed, but with the help of another grandmaster named Hideo Yamamura, he fully recovered from his injury.

When I met Arthur, his energy and the way he spoke gave me a hope I had never known. I just knew this guy was going to have a major impact on my life. In that first session I learnt about visualisation and the power of positive thoughts, and my mind opened up to a whole new world of possibility.

The session left me drained, though, and so after a nap at the hotel we headed off to meet everyone at Sawtell Pizza for a feed before we hit the pub for the kick-off party of the weekend. The beers went down a lot better this time and everyone was having a good laugh. I got to catch up with everyone I hadn't seen in the previous four months and also personally thank them all for the good wishes and support. I could tell a lot of people didn't really know how to react. It was just as new to them as it was for me, a learning experience, but after a few drinks we all picked up where we left off and it felt so good to be reunited with everyone. A lot of those people bought me a beer, and after being off them for so long the night turned into a bit of a blur.

The next morning the nurse came bright and early. Considering how much I'd had to drink, I was feeling pretty good. I think it was because I was so pumped for a day at the beach watching the comp. We got down to the beach around ten o'clock to see the tents in the front of the surf club packed with people.

Wow, Tubby you are the man! All these people had come out for me and I was speechless. The waves looked amazing and it was awesome to just hang out on the beach in the sun, watch everyone surf and catch up with more people I hadn't seen the night before. The boys brought Kirra down as well, and I loved having her by my side for it all.

We all planned to meet again that night down at the pub, but again the day had really taken it out of me, so I needed an afternoon nap to recharge. It turned out to be another fun night, with everyone in a great mood and the good times running high.

Sunday was finals day for the event, which again was a perfect day. Then followed the presentation at the Sawtell pub. The place was packed before the presentation had even started. They called me up to the front so I could say something to the crowd. I looked down to everyone, and that's when the reality of the event, and who had organised it, really hit me. I was overwhelmed with so much gratitude and as I went to speak I broke down crying in front of everyone. The previous few months had been really tough, and all the times I reached a point of wondering how I was going to cope through it, I would receive a card, a phone call or a visit – all from the people standing in front of me now. It was them who were helping me through it all and I couldn't believe that everyone in the room was here for me and had my back through this new journey I was on. It was proof right there that I was part of something pretty special, a community, the greatest community of Sawtell.

The Barney Miller Charity Surf Classic has just held its eighteenth annual event. After the first one helped me and showed me the gift of kindness and compassion in the hardest times, I chose to keep it running as an annual event and donate 100 per cent of the proceeds made over the weekend from auction items, raffles and competitors' entry fees, to a different recipient each year who has had a life-changing injury. This event gave me hope when I needed it and it is an honour to share that same hope with others. Our incredible community of Sawtell comes together for that weekend every year and everyone involved donates their time to help make it successful. The event is run by the Sawtell Boardriders Club and we bring in judges from around the state to keep it honest and fair for the competitive scoring. We have competitors come from all over the coast, some who have even gone on to qualify for the World Tour. Over the past eighteen years I am proud to have helped raise over a hundred thousand dollars combined for the recipients and I look forward to continually growing it in hope of supporting more individuals and their families.

* * *

It was sad saying goodbye to everyone. I so badly wanted to stay but it was nice to know it wouldn't be long till I would be home for good.

'I have amazing friends, Mum!' I cried as we boarded the plane to fly back to Sydney.

'Yes you do, and like me they will be there by your side on your road to recovery,' Mum replied with a tear rolling down her cheek.

When we landed we caught a cab out to Moorong. It was strange being back. It seemed a lot duller and bleaker than usual but it couldn't take away the feeling of hope that had swelled in me from everyone back home. It was suddenly clear to me that my true healing wouldn't really start until I was out of that place.

CHAPTER 10

WELCOME HOME, BARNEY

BARNEY

While I was in Moorong, I opted to have surgery to insert an indwelling suprapubic catheter. Instead of having it inserted through my penis, it went directly through my bladder wall into my upper pubic region. There are a lot of upsides to having it: lower risk of infection, painless erections, plus as a young male the ability to continue to have sex normally was pretty high up there on the pros-and-cons checklist. One of the main concerns for it, though, was always making sure it was not stabbing into me, constantly adjusting it into the right position for clear flow and double-checking it wasn't pulling down. In the beginning, I had it connected and free-flowing into a leg bag, but I was a surfer from the coast; I lived in boardies and I didn't want the world seeing my pee, so I set another goal: to recognise when I needed to go to the toilet and be able to cap off the tube. Truthfully, there were a few accidents along the way; I figured the only way to really feel it was to cap it off and let my bladder fill up and get used to the sensation. At first I would just leave it off for a short time and empty it regardless of how long or little time had passed. I gradually stretched it out and would try to wait for a sensation or a signal hoping my body would tell me when I needed to go. I guess it's kind of the same as teaching a toddler to recognise the signals. Eventually it clicked, so now when I need to pee I have a valve at the end of my catheter tube that switches on and off, and that's it.

After six months of rehab in Moorong I finally got to go home. I had met a girl named Lisa, who was friends with my cousin and was studying to be an occupational therapist. It had definitely crossed my mind that the chances of meeting someone who could love me regardless of my current situation was small, but I also had friends with nothing physically wrong with them who had trouble finding someone, so it felt good to know that I was one of the lucky ones. We were together for two years and even though it didn't last, I will always be grateful to Lisa for showing me that I am worth loving. She helped in making the transition of coming home into my new normality a lot easier to cope with and we shared some great memories.

* * *

Not long before we moved home, Mum and Mal were married in a nice ceremony at Cremorne Point overlooking Sydney Harbour. My house was now like the Brady Bunch: our home had been renovated from the two-bedroom beach shack it once was, into a two-storey house, big enough to fit all my new siblings. So much had changed yet it also felt the same. I had the same great friends I had always had, plus I was beginning to gain new ones. I never wanted to get comfortable in my chair, but I was happy to adapt and help make things easier and better for my family and friends.

For the 2000 Sydney Olympics I was nominated to carry the torch for our town. This was probably one of the coolest perks of my injury and an honour I will always be proud of. My leg of the torch run was the exact three-quarter mark around Australia and it even made it to the big screen of the Opening Ceremony while Tina Arena sang 'The Flame'. My sister Lara was working in athlete services for both the Olympics and Paralympics and got us tickets to watch the wheelchair rugby and basketball. It certainly was an experience. I knew almost immediately that it wasn't for me but I appreciated my family's gesture in trying to show me the other side of this injury. Wheelchair sports was never really my thing, but I highly respect the people who do go down that path. Everyone has their own journey.

* * *

Things had been going well, I was continuing my rehab at home and getting back into the swing of life. I was still dedicated to getting back on my feet but after my break-up with Lisa, I didn't quite have the same focus. I was hanging out with the few boys who were left in town as often as I could, always wanting to keep the party alive. I had a caregiver who would help with my daily needs and take me to appointments, supervised by a head registered nurse. The one in charge of my program always made his opinions known, continually lecturing me about dealing with my supposedly inevitable depression. He believed that it was unhealthy for me to be constantly hanging out with my mates to avoid the unavoidable. I have this automatic reflex, though, that kicks in the moment someone who doesn't really know me or have my best interests at heart tries to tell me who I am, how I should feel or what I can do. It may sound arrogant but I think it's really just the athlete in me or the male ego. He needed to go; I could no longer have someone around me who was constantly judging my behaviour and not allowing me to simply be whatever it was I needed to be at that time. Life is one long learning process, and I really believe that everything happens when it is supposed to. It's about timing.

To be honest, depression always seemed like the worst option for me. My life was already in a place I didn't want it to be, so I always chose to put my energy into healing and things that made me happy. It definitely helped being surrounded by people who made me laugh and it was those types of people who got me through.

I got a call from my lawyer to tell me that the date had been set for my court case. It had been a few years since we first started building the case and after that time, my team was confident that we had a strong enough case to win. It's always intimidating speaking in detail to anyone of official status. Luckily for me, my grounds for the law suit were self-explanatory. I was, after all, paralysed in a wheelchair and could barely move my arms enough to push myself. After three emotionally draining days we came to an agreement. Although money could never buy what I had lost, thanks to my incredible legal team I was compensated enough to help me move forward. Soon after, I employed a financial advisor to help me manage and budget my funds. We made a few successful investments early on, which helped set me up for my future. I don't really like talking about money, but I want to take this time to put into context the importance this has had on my life. I consider myself one of the lucky ones. A lot of people are not compensated when they have a life-altering injury or disease strike them. They are left to refinance their homes, sell everything and even go back to work at jobs that put their health at risk. Again, I consider myself lucky that I was young and single with no kids. I can't imagine how hard it would be to juggle it all with a family, and I really admire the people who pull it together and just make it work because I know it's neither easy nor cheap. Money, or lack of, is often the third wheel in relationships and why a lot of them end. I guess I am just saying that I am grateful that I have been given the means to support myself through this life and I appreciate its value. It is also why I now dedicate my life to getting back on my feet and showing the world what is possible. I was given this chance and I'm not going to waste it. It really upsets me that sometimes the difference between someone getting the right help they need and not getting it is money. I hope one day I can help bridge that gap and help people to see that our health should not be based on our bank balance, but simply be seen as a human right.

* * *

Mal was a draftsman, and the plan was to eventually build a home for me to move into, so we were excited when a property came on the market across the road from theirs. I was nervous on auction day because I really wanted it. The location was perfect and the white house sat on the top street side of the block with a backyard that backed on to the creek with ocean views. I ended up in a bidding war with another guy and as I reached near my limit he came in hitting it. I ended up putting in an extra $500 and managed to win. I couldn't believe how close I had come to losing the auction, but it was mine.

My plan to begin with was to rent the place out to friends while we worked on the design plans and financing – but in reality it turned into two years of parties. We hosted birthdays, New Year's Eve, pre-parties and after-parties. It was a pretty crazy time. After discussing plans for the new place with Mal, we agreed that the block wasn't going to be the best fit for me because of its downward angle towards the back of the yard. It was fine temporarily but the idea was to make it more accessible. We decided that instead of building one house for me, we would build two townhouses, one down the bottom on the water and one at the top, street side. The top one would be mine to continue to rent out, and the bottom one would be a place designed for Mum and Mal and his daughters to have, and I would keep the original house on the corner, which was already set up for me. Mal drew up the plans, submitted them to council and everything was ready to go.

I spent some time travelling around with some friends who were in a band called One Dollar Short. I managed to see their show twenty-two times over six months, with a few shows ending with me on stage singing along to the crowds. When the annual Barney Miller Classic was approaching I invited One Dollar Short to play. The night, at the Sawtell RSL, was massive, and then we had one last after-party before demolition day. Everything had been cleared from the house days prior, except for a sign we got from our mate Kobus that read 'BORONIA STREET BOOZE BARN'. The empty house and backyard – even the street – were soon filled with lots of people for what turned into a legendary night worthy of that sign.

As the house was getting underway, the time came for me to buy a car. It was a brand-new Chrysler Grand Voyager. I bought it from the local dealer in Coffs Harbour and scheduled for it to be modified into a fully accessible van by a company in Queensland. I had a mate drive it up and drop it off to them for the fit-out, which took four weeks to complete, and then another mate drove Kobus and me to pick it up. When we arrived one of the workers came over to run through how it all worked. With either the press of a button or a slight opening of the side sliding door, the car would lower and a ramp on the passenger side would automatically fold out. The back bench seats stayed in place but the middle two seats were removable to make space for my wheelchair to enter. I decided to have the middle seats removed because the majority of the time I would be staying in my chair, while we drove around town. Long trips, I opted to sit in the front passenger seat to be more secure and comfortable. There was also an option to remove either the front passenger seat or even the driver's seat if I wanted to drive, but I chose to keep them in place. After a long demonstration of all of the modifications, it was time for Kobus and me to hit the road back to Sawtell so we could make it back in time to meet up with everyone at the Coffs Harbour RSL. I think it was someone's birthday, but honestly we didn't need an excuse to go out. Back then it was about a six-hour drive; I sat in the front passenger seat and we left just after lunch and got home in good time. We made a stop at Kobus's house to pick up his sister who was our designated driver for the night and a few boys met us there to head into town. It was another fun night out, but every night was fun with this crew. At the end of the night we all piled into the van to head home. This time I stayed in my chair while another mate jumped into the front passenger seat. He launched up pretty quickly, complaining that the seat was burning him, but we were all pretty drunk, so we laughed it off.

The following morning when my nurse arrived for my morning routine she noticed I had broken blisters on my bum. After my shower she dressed them and told me to try to stay off it as much as I could. Thanks to the night before I was happy to hang out in bed all day.

I didn't have a great amount of sensation back then, which was why I didn't realise that I had actually been burned by the passenger seat in my new van. After having a flat battery in the car a few times, we sent it to an auto electrician to figure out what was happening. I had flashbacks of my mate saying how hot the seat was on the way home from the bar, and I had been sitting in that seat for six hours. Thinking back, I did feel uncomfortable but I put it down to nerve pain. I also took any feeling as good feeling, which was why I never complained about it. We began to piece each piece of the puzzle together to come to the realisation that the car had been rewired incorrectly under the seat during the modifications. The passenger-seat heater was wired directly to the car battery, which was draining it over and over again and why my seat was boiling and my bum was burnt. These burns – which were on each cheek – turned out to be third-degree burns that had to be dressed daily by a community nurse. It was so serious I ended up having to spend the next ten months laid out on my stomach, and doing all my bathroom routines of toileting and showers hoisted up in a sling so I didn't put any pressure on the wounds.

My first reaction was that it was fine, it should be sorted out in a few weeks. Then month after month went by and it still hadn't healed. This time brought another reminder of how awesome my friends are. They often moved the party to my room. It was kind of like déjà vu: rehab all over again yet in my own home. I had recently taken over the rapid rafting business I used to work for and so my days were now all about rosters, staff and bookings. I loved it because it kept me busy and gave me a sense of responsibility and normality that helped make the time go by. I occasionally found myself frustrated with how long it was taking to heal but if I had learnt anything from my spinal injury, it was patience. The hardest part was not being able to do my physical therapy.

After seven months of basically lying face-down, I had the opportunity to see Christopher Reeve speak about the future of spinal-cord injuries. But in terms of preparing for the trip, it was as if I had gone backwards a few years. I had to have loads of cushioned pressure pads underneath me, and because it was an overnight trip I was only allowed to go to the event and then get off my bum as soon as I could. Christopher Reeve was such a legend. He was the real superman in every way possible. He spoke so positively about his fight to find a cure. It was an honour to hear him speak and to this day I am grateful to have simply been in his presence.

Ten months finally passed and I was allowed to start transitioning back into my chair. I had to begin with a multi-layered cushion and slowly got to work my way back to a normal one after a few more months. When I think back to that time I actually find it hard to remember how I got through it all without losing my mind. Internet was still scarce and my mobile phone was a Nokia 6210. But still as every day rolled into the next, I never lost my spirit, and again I attribute that to my awesome family and friends for never giving up on me.

CHAPTER 11

OCEAN HEALING

BARNEY

My parents' place across the road was finished and they were ready to move over. Usually it's the child who moves out, but this time I made the parents leave. I was excited to live independently and I knew that if I ever did need them that they were only across the road.

I had some friends, Quinny, Timmy and Hannah, move in with me, which made things lively. My house had three additional bedrooms upstairs and a shared bathroom. The kitchen and laundry were downstairs for all of us to share. What made it work and so fun was that we had all known each other for a while and had the same circle of friends. They were so easy to live with and looked after the house.

My new housemates were awesome with Kirra, and she loved them as well. In fact, she loved them so much that she would sneak out with them and follow them without them knowing. Next thing the boys would be at a bar ordering their first drink and look down to see Kirra at their side sitting there wagging her tail and looking up at them.

The thing about beagles is that they are incredibly smart in a mischievous way. Kirra had everyone working for her and if they weren't on her program she made them know that she was always one step ahead. Throughout the history of the Booze Barn another mate who lived with me on multiple occasions, Milka, fell victim many times to her antics. She didn't like it when he roused on her, so she would let herself upstairs sometimes and either rip up rubbish or on one occasion out of the blue she left three turds on his bed. This was hilarious to everyone but him.

The summer before, we had started a thing called the Summer Shed Series, in which we would all drink down in the shed/gym where I would work out on a Friday afternoon. Everyone would meet there before all heading out in town.

The parties continued in the New Booze Barn. The garage had an open deck, which was the perfect place for a party and could fit a lot of people. Sometimes they would cause a bit of trouble in the neighbourhood and it wasn't a rare sight to see police cars turn up. We had many great parties, including the annual Christmas Santa Party, where everyone would dress as Santa, and the Green Dress Party which was named after our housemate Hannah's favourite green Supré dress. We also loved a good fireworks show and would often host our own out of the shed. So many memories of wild nights and good times.

I wished the first lot of friends who moved in never left, because the house would have stayed in a lot better shape, but as life happens people move on to new things. But not for me. As friends moved on or moved away the younger crew would become my new drinking buddies. Everyone likes to joke that when I had my accident, I got stuck as a twenty-year-old, well for eight years, anyway.

Party after party, drink after drink for years. The house copped a flogging and of course so did my health.

Over the years I also hired many different mates as my carer. Marto, Grohl, Penfold, Tubby, Beno, Unit, Parko and Luke. It was awesome because it was just like hanging out. I was lucky enough to have good mates who cared enough to take on the job.

I was training twice a week with a personal trainer and I would also get on the Motomed – a motorised cycle machine – most days to move my legs. I would also have a massage every week. All the exercise I was doing back then was pretty much so I didn't feel guilty about going out and drinking on the weekend.

There was a six-month period in which I would buy a bottle of Jägermeister on Friday afternoons and smash down Jäger bombs with a couple of mates, then call a cab and go into town. Then drink copious amounts of Jäger bombs at the bar. There was an establishment that stayed open until almost sunrise, so often we would roll home in the early daylight. If a mate wasn't with me I'd get a cab home by myself, and eventually I got to know the cabbies, some of whom would even help me inside and help me into bed. The next morning I would wake up for the nurse, spend the day in bed and rest, then do it all again that night to then wake up Sunday morning to the nurse and a two-day hangover.

I kept telling myself that I was here to have a good time, but I think everyone knew the truth was that I was just avoiding all the things I hated about my life. Every now and then after way too much alcohol, something would tip me off and I would break down and cry to whoever was with me. I so desperately didn't want to be treated differently, I wanted everyone to know that I was still the same as I had always been. I felt like I had a reputation to uphold and a point to prove that I could still hang out and keep up. I think I just took it overboard a few too many times.

I was more focused on what we were doing on the weekend than on myself and my therapy, and I was beginning to scare my family and friends. My mum especially was worried because she knew how determined I was to get better. Most of my close friends, the ones who weren't scared to tell me to pull my head in, had moved away to pursue their lives. I think that was another underlying issue, which I drowned in alcohol. I had so many plans to travel, but I was stuck. I loved Sawtell but I knew there was so much more out there for me.

Things began to take a turn for the better when my mate Parko became my carer. It was awesome, because his job was to pretty much just hang out with me and take me to my appointments. He also came along when I finally got to take an overseas trip. (Well, it was my second trip overseas; the first was when I was fourteen and my mum won a trip to Vanuatu for the two of us.) I had got talking to one of the older boys of Sawtell about his travels, and he invited me to go with him to Thailand. I was pumped about the idea, but as usual we had to work out all the logistics. I took Parko and my nurse, Carla, along for the ten-day trip, which was a pretty big deal for me, but I was ready to get out and immerse myself into another culture.

We flew into Bangkok and spent a few nights exploring the city and eating some of the best food I have had. We then drove to the south-east coast to spend a night in Pattaya.

Next we caught a ferry to the secluded island of Koh Chang, where we spent five nights. It looked and felt like paradise, and we were treated like kings. We had massages on the beach, incredible food, and the staff were very friendly and happily accommodated my needs. In fact, the most important thing I learnt about the Thai people on my trip is that they are very determined to make you feel welcome.

Thailand gave me a taste of all the things I was missing out on, and I couldn't wait to plan my next trip.

* * *

My best mate, Toby Webber, came to visit not long after I got home from Thailand. Whenever we caught up we would always go up to the headland and watch the surf together. We got talking about how much I missed it and wanted to get back out there. For a long time I had it in my head that the only way I could surf again was how I used to. In the beginning I couldn't bear the thought of the love of my life – surfing – being compromised and adapted. I thought I wouldn't feel the same rush that I once did when I could stand. But the thing was, not being out there at all was a worse alternative. We started to brainstorm ideas to help me surf again. Toby and the boys had been planning a trip to America, starting in Hawaii around December, so I decided to go with them. Plus I was pretty stoked about going to see the world famous Pipe in real life. This gave me something to look forward to.

I had only been back in the ocean a handful of times. And I was scared. I was scared of it being different, I was scared of it swallowing me whole. I had actually developed a fear of swimming over the previous few years. I had learnt to float and do backstroke and even hold my breath to swim under water, but during one hydrotherapy session, when Toby was with me and talking to my physio as I swam around, I came up from below the water to take a breath but didn't come up far enough. I took in water instead of air and started to choke. I suddenly went limp and didn't have the strength to call attention or turn over. As each second passed I drifted further and further away from being able to hold on. I began to panic, thinking, *This is it, this is how it ends for me*. I remember the bubbles at the surface getting brighter and brighter, like the white light was beginning to shine through. I must have been seconds away from losing consciousness when they pulled me up and out of the water. Toby said my face was blue. It was a close one, that's for sure, and I didn't realise how much it had affected me until we started to plan my return to the surf. Everything was going to be different, but all I wanted was to see if it gave me even a glimpse of the feeling that it used to. I also trusted my mates, who would be out there with me, so that was enough to help me face those fears.

Growing up, we had all watched surf movies of the Pipe Masters, and it was such a trip to know that we were going to witness it in person. This time I was going with Parko and Toby, and also our mates Hiddo and Joey. It was a learning process, in every new place we visited, in what my needs were, but I managed to find a nursing service to help with my morning routine and the boys helped out with the rest. We arrived in Honolulu and drove out to the iconic North Shore. We had rented a house at Sunset Beach and we were so pumped for the following twelve days. It was the first time to America for all of us, so driving on the other side of the road took a bit of getting used to, but we had a great time exploring the island, swimming and snorkling. I hung out on the beach a lot soaking up the sun and watching the boys surf. We heard the announcement that the legendary Eddie Aikau Big Wave Contest was going to run for the first time in a few years, which was a dream come true to see that wave in action in real life. As the swell grew the crashing of the waves rumbled the ground, sometimes even washing up onto the streets.

Another bucket-list moment came as we sat on the beach in front of Pipe. For those who have no idea what Pipeline is, it is one of the most powerful waves in the world where surfers risk their lives to compete and conquer the wave. It is the final stop of the World Surfing Tour each year. It was even bigger and scarier in person than it was in the magazines, but it was just so cool to experience it all with my mates I had grown up with. We had dreamt of being here since we were kids, and after my accident, there was a strong possibility that it might never have happened, so it was extra special to be there and in the presence of the greatest surfers on the planet.

We were invited to the Gerry Lopez Volcom house to watch the contest. I was losing it inside that I was actually in the famous house that has been shot in the background of Pipe in numerous magazines and videos. I was so excited to watch the contest. We met a guy named Jesse Billauer, a quadriplegic from Southern California who was back surfing again. We didn't get to talk about boards, but he told me to get in touch via email.

As we boarded the flight home, I knew that Hawaii had become a part of me, and that I wanted to spend that time of the year there every year for as long as I could. I left feeling re-energised and focused on the new task at hand: to get back in the surf.

After emailing Jesse with questions he replied that his board was eight foot two inches. I still had a few more things to work out but I had seen from footage that he also had straps two-thirds of the way up the board to prop himself up onto his elbows, which helped steer him across the wave.

I approached a local shaper whom I had known for years, Tony Derbyshire, to custom design a surfboard for me. He was immediately excited by the project, and we got started on design ideas. It was a totally new field for him to play in and all new learning for me. All we had to go off was my description of Jesse on his board and the fact that it was eight foot two. We talked about my weight and height, and what I was hoping to achieve on the board. Did I want to just ride the wave straight in like a surf-school board, or did I want to learn manoeuvres? So many extra details compared to a regular custom stand-up short board. I had to consider if I was going to strap my legs together or let my feet just hang over the edge. Then there was deck grip to keep me from sliding backwards and forwards on the board. We played around with ideas for months until we found the perfect design plan.

The surfing bug had truly bitten me, so I booked another trip. This time Parko and I went to Jeffreys Bay in South Africa. The Billabong Pro was on and we were again psyched to see some world-class surfing. The trip to Hawaii had reinforced my love for not only the ocean and surfing but the competition. There was something about being in the atmosphere of diehard surf fans that inspired me. It reminded me that I was also a diehard surf fan and although I could no longer compete or – in the meantime – surf, I still wanted and needed to be around that energy. I had missed that feeling.

South Africa was very different from Hawaii, but I couldn't help but fall in love with the place. It had many contrasts and elements I had never been exposed to before. The difference between wealth and poverty was a huge one. One of the highlights of the trip was going on a safari tour. It was insane to see the animals in their habitats. It really is upsetting that people find pleasure in hunting these beautiful creatures.

The other highlight was of course the surf contest. For what is usually a small sleepy beach town, Jeffreys Bay comes to life during the event and is covered with tourists from all over the world. It was so busy that whenever I tried to find a place to view the surf action, people would stand in front of me blocking my view. One of the surfers on tour walked past and noticed I was having a hard time seeing. He came and introduced himself – it was Mick Fanning, who is now a triple world champion surfer and surfing legend. He took Parko and me in to sit with him in the competitors' area. We got chatting about my injury and his injury that he had come back from earlier that year. His was pretty gnarly as well. He had torn his hamstring off the bone and his surgeon reset it with a screw.

Even though we had totally different injuries and of course mine was more complicated, hearing that his odds of returning to peak condition for competitive surfing were slim and that he was going to go for it anyway – well, it was the start of a great mateship and a new source of inspiration.

I told Mick of my plans to get back in the surf and about the surfboard being shaped for me. He was so stoked for me and so quick to help. He put me in contact with the former team manager at Rip Curl and through him the company was kind enough to give me some wetsuits; it was the beginning of my twelve-year-and-counting relationship with Rip Curl.

Not long after we got home, Tony called to tell me that my custom board was almost ready. I needed to go in to lie on the board and get a feel for where things were going to go. I could also test out the Velcro pockets that would support my elbows and help me steer, and the kick pads on either side that would hold my hips in place on the board.

The hardest part was now having to wait for my return trip to Hawaii. That's where I had set the goal for my first surf.

Another step forward was getting my licence back. When my diagnosis was made, my licence was suspended, and now I had to go back through the whole system again. I had to take the written test for my learner's permit, which shockingly took me three times because the rules had obviously changed a lot since I originally got my licence. (I also didn't read the study book they gave me, which I am sure would have helped.) After six months of lessons and learning to drive with my hands instead of my feet, I took the driver's test and passed. I had just bought myself a new black Holden SS Crewman Ute, and I was hanging out to drive it. Holden installed hand controls in the car for me – push down to accelerate and push forward to break – which were connected to the regular foot pedals so anyone else could still drive it. I also had a removable handle put on the steering wheel to help me steer. It took a bit of getting used to driving my new way but it felt good to be back behind the wheel again – but not enough to be the designated driver.

I invited a mate, Penfold, to come to Hawaii with me this time. He was one of my past carers and I was excited to show him the place that had reunited me with surfing. I called Mick Fanning to let him know we had arrived and to keep me posted on when worked best for him and the boys to take me surfing. The following day I woke up in our rented house at Keiki Beach to a text from Mick saying the contest was off for the day and they were keen to take me out.

This was it. I was all kinds of anxious and excited, but mostly ready. I just couldn't wait to feel the wave pick me up and to be free out there. It was independence. There was no chair and I would finally be sharing waves with the boys again. Mick told us to meet him at the Rip Curl house, which was located right on Pipe. We got there and the boys were all psyching. Mick gave me a hug and asked if I was ready to surf Pipe. I remember freaking out initially but then thought of how much the young

Barney would have been losing his mind at the opportunity to surf one of the most iconic waves in the world.

We geared up and headed down to the beach. This was everyone's first time doing this, but as surfers we have an instinct of what works and what doesn't. It was basically like taking a learner surfer out for the first time. We had Mick pushing me with flippers and the rest of the boys spread out all over the line-up to be ready to catch me at any moment.

The set was coming and everyone started to cheer and call me onto the wave, and with one big push I was on it. It didn't matter that it was different from how I used to do it. It still gave me the same rush and the same feelings it always had. It was pure healing, euphoric energy.

I came home on such a high. I'd forgotten how one wave could totally erase a bad day. How a fun surf could totally change your week or, in my case, years. I know I have said it a lot and I will keep saying it till the end of time: my friends are fucking awesome. They have helped me more than they will ever know; getting me back to the surf, travelling with me, putting up with my crazy drunken songwriting days (definitely not in Kate's league – but I'd write a few alcohol-fuelled tunes for my mates). My friends have been my backbone and not for a second let me believe that I was any less than before my accident. I got through all of it because of them.

But speaking of friends, everyone knows that dogs are a man's best friend and my beagle Kirra, she was the best. She was getting a little slower, but mind you if she wanted to run to say hi to another dog or if she heard the word 'Dinner!', she would find that pep in her step. Her breathing was getting a bit louder, but the vet assured us it was nothing to be concerned about; as dogs get older the palate at the back of their tongue gets softer and starts to vibrate. I thought that if I got another puppy it might give Kirra a second wind and she could mother it and teach it her ways, though hopefully not the mischievous ones. I started to look at bulldogs because they are not too crazy and pretty chilled, so it would suit Kirra perfectly. I'd found a male British bulldog about three hours' drive south, but because he was only six weeks old we couldn't pick him up for another two weeks. I was so excited to give Kirra a little friend. Just three days before we were due to pick him up, Kirra's breathing got even louder. I took her to the vet for her yearly check-up and X-rays, and this time they came back with bad news.

I was really emotional when I got to the vet: scared, confused and wondering what the hell was going on.

I went into the room with the vet and Kirra. He said the scan came back showing growths of cancer in her lungs and stomach and that there was not much they could do. 'If she were younger we could have operated, but being twelve I'm not sure if she'd make it through. It's up to you though,' he said.

He told me she was suffering, so my choice was to risk putting her through the surgery or to put her to sleep. My heart broke instantly and I told him I couldn't do it. He said, 'Well, how about you take her home and think about it, then let me know what you want to do.'

I held her tight the whole way home, willing her to hang in there. But dogs have an innate way of knowing when it's their time, and over those three days Kirra went downhill fast.

Two nights later she kept wandering around the house, and her breathing was so loud it kept me awake. She came to a stop and lay at the front door, which was right outside my bedroom window, and she was panting so loudly that I started to cry. 'It's okay, Kirra,' I kept saying in between the tears. 'You're a good girl.'

I couldn't let her live like this anymore. And as I continued to cry I told myself it was the right decision for her. The following morning I called the vet and said I was going to bring Kirra in. I lay with her all morning on my bed and then we put her on my lap in the car, with me holding onto her so tightly as we drove in. Mum and my sister Tania met us outside the vet and I broke down and cried, 'I can't.'

I gave her one last squeeze, kissed her goodbye and told her thank you and that I loved her. Watching her walk away and through those doors with Mum and Tania broke my heart. If it wasn't for that fact that I was picking up my new puppy in the afternoon I honestly would have fallen apart.

I know a lot of people might think: it's just a dog, why were you so upset? But imagine this: you have a dog for over twelve years and in that time you've probably been away from them a handful of times. There's not another single person you have spent that amount of time with. They are there by your side always, all they ever think about when you're not there is you. Their whole world is you. They are as much a part of your family as you are.

Having a dog taught me so many of life's lessons and values as a kid. I was in charge of this puppy's life; I fed her, walked her, gave her my attention and cleaned up after her. The one thing we can all learn from a dog is that all we really need in this world is love. If we can give love and be open to receive love, life can be amazing.

CHAPTER 12

STARS ALIGNED

KADA

A few weeks had passed and the reality that I no longer lived with my family began to sink in. Mostly I was happy with my new life, but I couldn't help but feel that this newfound happiness was only a mask covering up my scars. I turned to Richard's mum, Cathy, a lot for advice; she had a way of making me feel better and helping me see the bigger picture.

My plan was to continue my hairdressing apprenticeship but after going to multiple salons there were no opportunities open for me. So I put my résumé out, hoping and waiting to get a job in retail at the Plaza for the time being.

I had made a decision that this was my time. A time to work on myself and get to know me. No boys, no distractions, just me. Well, that plan lasted all of a few weeks.

It was the annual Sawtell Chilli Festival. Every year vendors from all around Australia come to showcase their best chilli products, which range from hot sauces to chilli beer and chilli chocolate. Thousands of people walk the street that is closed off for the event and the energy is contagious; there is even a chilli-eating competition. I wasn't really much of a chilli fan back then but I made sure to try as much as I could handle. After doing the rounds of all the stalls I stopped in at the pub to meet up with a friend. That was when I saw him. He had a presence about him that I found really intriguing and his smile could light up a room. There was an instant connection that I couldn't explain, I just knew that he had a story and I wanted to know it. I could tell that there was more to him than what was in front of me. This guy knew life, he had lived and he was here to do nothing but enjoy it. He ever so cheekily yet politely introduced himself.

'I'm Barney. I haven't seen you around here before.'

I replied, 'I'm Kate, I just moved here a few weeks ago.'

As we got lost in conversation about everything from football to science, the thing that really struck a chord with me was his self-confidence. Well, he had been drinking, a lot, and that definitely helps give a good boost, but it was what he said to me that made me know he was different. He was older than me and clearly had lived through things I never would. When I asked him what had happened to him and if he was going to be in the wheelchair forever, his reply was full of certainty. He said, 'No, this is not forever, I'll find a way.' He told me it had been eight years since his accident and how even though it changed the way he did things, it hadn't changed him. If anything, he was out to prove that he could still keep up with everyone, if not do it better. I really admired that about him.

I said my goodbyes in a bit of a daze and walked home. What had just happened? What was it about him that had me looking at my life and choices and finally seeing that none of it mattered? I now had the independence that I had been searching for but it had come at a price: I was now ten hours drive away from my family. Barney just wanted the independence to run down to the beach to check the surf, to go to the bathroom, to take care of himself. I suddenly felt guilty at the selfishness and shallowness I had fallen victim to.

That big picture that Cathy was always talking to me about was finally starting to make sense. I remember having a breakthrough of sheer regret. For every horrible thing I had ever said to my family, who did nothing but love me. For the choices I made to satisfy my needs without thinking of the consequences. Why did I have to live so far away from my family in order to have a better relationship with them? These were all the questions that were triggered after meeting

Barney. How was he so okay? Why wasn't he mad? Because I was mad. I was mad at where my life had taken me, and that it was purely from my poor choices. He was hurt by someone else's poor choice and it totally changed his life.

This was a huge breakthrough for me. I had always found an excuse for my behaviour – there was always something or someone else to blame – but for the first time I saw my faults and I was open to accepting them. Something about my conversation with Barney had made me want to believe that there was hope for everyone.

A few weeks later, I received a call from my cousin Gabby to let me know that a close friend of ours, Marc, had been hit by a motorbike at traffic lights. I remember trying to stay calm and collected, but when she called back a few hours later to tell me he was gone, I was shattered. Marc was one of the most kind-hearted souls, and I was blessed to have shared a piece of his short life.

The next day I went down to the beach to clear my head. That is where I saw him again. Barney was with a friend checking the surf. He was in his 4WD beach chair. I saw him first before he saw me and I contemplated turning my head and walking the other way because I was kind of a mess. I also had a slight fear that if I said hi, he wouldn't remember me because the last time we spoke he'd been drunk. I did want to talk to him, though, so I headed towards him. We locked eyes and he called out to me. I walked over to him and his friend, Nigel, and we talked briefly about the weather and all those clichéd subjects you bring up when you don't really know what to say. Then he asked if I was going to the Coffs Cup Race Day. I didn't want to tell him I was actually underage, so I just said, 'Oh, I don't know, it's not really my thing.' He then asked what I was doing for work and I told him I was on the hunt for a hairdressing apprenticeship or maybe a job in retail if I couldn't do that.

We ended the conversation with him asking for my phone number. As he tapped it into his phone and went to save it, he looked up at me and said, 'It's . . . Amanda, isn't it?' I laughed and said, 'Um no, it's Kate.' I should have been offended but I wasn't. I found it funny that he just went for a name and hoped for the best. I mean, it worked – we are here telling this story ten years later.

* * *

Everything always seems worse at night. I remember calling my mum to talk about Marc and the funeral details and just breaking down. I didn't know how much more heartache I could take. I remember getting pretty worked up, crying hysterically that life wasn't fair. Apparently my last words to her before I hung up were: 'I just don't want to deal with it anymore.' I didn't realise how terrifying those words would be for a mother who was ten hours drive away, but I just meant I was going to break my dedication to sobriety and have a drink. I told myself it was for Marc but deep down I knew it was for me. For me to cope with the next few days.

It was the middle of winter, so the sun set early. After a few hours contemplating if I would just sleep on it or drown my sorrows, I decided to go out for a walk. I made it only a few steps when I ran into Nigel, Barney's friend from the beach. He had been at the races all day with Barney and he was about to catch a cab home so he could prepare for his trip to America the following day. My phone had run out of credit and died, so I borrowed a phone from my roommate, Rachel, to message Barney and see what he was doing. He messaged back to say that he had just got home and a few people were heading over, and he invited me to join them. Rachel knew how devastated I had been about Marc, so she came along to keep an eye on me.

We arrived at the notorious Booze Barn to loud roars of laughter. Barney was already in bed but was up watching TV. We passed a few people on the way in and they pointed me in the direction of Barney's bedroom. I didn't know where to sit but he insisted I sit next to him on the bed. As we talked and laughed about anything and everything, the connection I had felt the previous times we had spoken was again strong. Rachel came to say goodbye and I told her I wouldn't be home too late. When she closed the door behind her, I turned back to continue the conversation – then he kissed me. It was different from how I had ever been kissed. It was a kiss to say,

Everything is and will be okay. We stopped and looked at each other and laughed again. It didn't feel awkward or weird, it felt as if I had known him my whole life. It felt perfect. We talked all night, so much that I fell asleep in his arms.

I woke in a panic the next morning. Rachel was probably worried, my phone was dead and I had to get ready for the funeral. I thanked Barney for a wonderful night and for giving me exactly what I needed. I got home and Rachel was out, so I put my phone on the charger while I got ready to face the day. When my phone turned on it rang almost immediately: it was my mum, who had been up all night worried about me and calling everyone she knew to find me. She finally got through to Rachel, who gave her Barney's number, and she called him not long after I had left. I realised my dramatics the day before had scared her sick. How could I have been so reckless yet have the best night of my life? I assured her that she had nothing to worry about, that I was okay and was going to be okay. The crazy thing was that this time I actually believed it when I said it.

The funeral was beautiful and the church where Marc found sanctuary was filled with hundreds of people, all there to pay their respects and celebrate his life. Despite the sadness of the occasion I couldn't help but think of my night with Barney and how simply perfect it was. I didn't yet understand the feeling I had. I was excited to see him again, so I texted him to say I was going to the pub for dinner and a game of pool and asked if he would like to join me.

When I met him down there he asked me if I wanted to go back to his place to watch a movie instead of dinner at the pub, and I accepted the invitation. It makes me giggle thinking about this next part. I asked him how we were going to get back to his place, should I call a cab? His house is literally a five-minute walk around the corner slightly up the hill. He laughed at me, called me cute and said, 'No, you have to push me.'

Push him? I'm not going to lie, I had no idea how to do it or if I could do it, but I laughed nervously and said, 'Okay!'

I'm sure I looked hilarious as I put all my might into pushing him up the hill, but we made it – only to have the next challenge thrown at me. Barney had a nine-month-old English bulldog named Jäger who was not at all sure about me taking away the attention of his favourite human. Rule number one: don't try to get down on the same level as a jealous bulldog. He toppled me over, trying to hump me to show his dominance. It was hilarious, and from that moment I was determined to win him over.

We then went inside into Barney's room to challenge number three: transferring Barney onto his bed. None of the boys were home yet, so it was up to me to make it happen. I was terrified of hurting him but after a few minutes of him reassuring me that he has taken many falls and this one would be an easy landing if it went wrong, I was ready to try. Barney could hardly move at this stage. His legs felt like dead weights and his upper body strength was basically non-existent, but his determination to make this work made up for it all. He made me believe that we were capable, so I trusted him. I lined his chair up to the side of the bed, then pulled his body forward in his chair and put each leg up on the bed. As I counted to three Barney launched his weight towards the bed as I scooped and rolled him. We did it. Now what?

He had an electric bed that adjusted to a sitting position, so after I got him comfortable we looked for a movie to watch. We chose *Transformers*, although there wasn't really much watching happening. I fell asleep in his arms again that night and woke up to the nurse arriving the next morning. I kissed him goodbye and left to head home.

Walking home, I had a warm fuzzy feeling. I had never had it before and I didn't want it to stop. There was something so honest and true about the connection I shared with Barney. He made me want to be better, he saw me for all that I am not all that I was. I kept replaying the past two nights in my head over and over and then I got a text from him saying, 'I'll call you later, beautiful.' I smiled with the peace of mind that came from having found something special. Even after such a short time, he made me truly happy.

CHAPTER 13

FINDING LOVE

BARNEY

It was with a heavy heart that I left the vet and drove the three hours south to pick up my new bulldog puppy, Jäger. Yeah, that was his name, because at the time Jägermeister was my drink of choice. (I can't handle the stuff now but it was fun while it lasted.)

It was pretty hard to stop crying, but I just kept pushing through and picked up a few of the boys on the way. I'd seen photos of the little guy and knew he was a little muscle ball of cuteness. We arrived in Taree and ended up going out for a few drinks to celebrate Kirra's life before we were due to pick up Jäger first thing the next morning. When we got to the club the security guard wouldn't let me in because my eyes were so red from crying that he thought I was on something more than alcohol. After watching the boys argue with him for a while I ended up telling him straight: 'Listen, mate, I had to put my dog to sleep today and I haven't been able to stop crying, so could you please let me in to have a couple of drinks?' He must have been a dog person because he told me he was sorry and let us go in.

The next morning when the bulldog breeder opened up the travel kennel I almost died because Jäger looked even cuter in real life than in the pictures. It helped a little with the pain of losing Kirra, but that first night when he cried a lot, I did too. If only Kirra were there to look after both of us!

From that day on he went everywhere with us. He became like one of the boys and was definitely used on several occasions to get the attention of girls. The bigger he got the more solid he got, and he soon grew into a little tank.

Nine months after Jäger came to live with us, it was the Sawtell Chilli Festival. For us it was a good excuse to sit on the deck of the pub, pound beers and watch the day go by – I couldn't have known that it would also change my life forever. I was sitting with a couple of mates when this island goddess came over to talk to one of the boys I was with. He introduced her as Kate. My confidence was high after a few drinks under my belt, so I sparked up a conversation asking how long she'd been here, because it's only a small place and I would have noticed that a girl of this calibre had moved to town. I asked where she was from and when she said, 'Cowra, you probably haven't heard of it,' I was able to humour her. My step-brother Tommy once had a girlfriend from Cowra, who turned out to be the older sister of one of Kate's good friends. Small world.

Well, that was that and we said our goodbyes and I forgot to get her number. Luckily a few weeks later I was down the beach at the Sawtell Surf Club when I saw her walk up the hill. She looked hesitant to come over, so I called out to her. After another nice chat I asked for her number. As I punched it into my phone I realised I couldn't remember her name, so I took a punt. 'It's Amanda, isn't it?'

I saw her face drop. 'It's Kate.'

Shit, I thought, but I texted her on the spot so she had my number.

Over the next couple of days I couldn't get her out of my head. Should I text her? Should I not text her? After a week of me procrastinating I got a text from her asking my plans for the next few days. I was excited to hear from her and started to text her back asking her to come to the races, and then . . . I got side-tracked. People who know me will tell you that this is totally normal for me; I often notice down the track that I have half-written replies to people who have texted me.

Coffs Cup Day started with a champagne – or let's just be honest and say it was Passion Pop – breakfast at my place, which included the staple food before going out and drinking: bacon-and-egg rolls. We then headed down to the main street and the boys lifted me into the bus to head into the Coffs racecourse, and whom did I see . . . Kate. I got excited, but then my enthusiasm shifted when she said, 'You didn't reply to me last night.'

Oh shit! I thought, and then I asked if she was coming to the races. I was disappointed when she said no, but I told her I would call her later. After our day at the races we went out in Coffs for a few hours and then headed home about eight o'clock. On the way home I received a text from an unknown number: *Hey, it's Kate. I'm on Rachel's phone. How was your day?* I rang the number straight back and Kate answered, so I told her a few people were coming over and invited her to join us.

I couldn't help but smile hugely when she arrived. I had gone to bed to watch a movie and asked her to join me. After a couple of drinks her friend Rachel came in to say goodbye, and when Kate's back was turned I decided that it was now or never, so as she turned back towards me I laid one on her lips. Boom! I think it stunned her, but I'm pretty sure she felt as happy as I did.

It was one of those moments in life where you just have to have a crack. Another saying I live by is: *You never know, unless you give it a go.* She could have shot me down in flames and who would know where my life would have gone – but I'm so glad she didn't. She ended up staying the night because we just got caught in the vortex of talking and next thing we knew the sun was coming up. I'd never ever done that before with someone, so obviously it was the right thing and the right someone.

The next morning she had to go to a funeral, so she took off. It was not long after she left I got a call from another unknown number.

'Where's my daughter?' was the first thing I heard.

'Sorry,' I replied. 'I missed that?'

'Where's Kathryn?'

I was still confused. 'Do you mean Kate?'

'No, it's *Kathryn*. Where is she?'

Ah, now it was a bit clearer, but the caller didn't sound happy.

'Ah, she just left to go home. Is this her mum?'

'Yes, I can't get through to her.'

'Don't worry,' I reassured her. 'She's safe. Her phone died but she should be home by now, so try ringing her in five.'

And that was that.

I sent Kate a text saying I was thinking about her at the funeral, and later that afternoon I bumped into her out the front of the Sawty Pub with a few friends.

When I asked her if she wanted to come back to my place to watch a movie, she agreed and asked how we would get there. Taxi?

I laughed and told her she would have to push me in my chair. I kind of threw her in the deep end because we lived up a hill, which I'm sure could have been a deal-breaker for some girls. But not Kate.

And it all just went from there. After hanging out for about a week I invited Kate to go with me to the Gold Coast for a night I had planned to catch up with a mate, and I was stoked that she was keen to come. We stayed with my mates, and I figured things were moving along nicely if I was introducing her to my friends.

We were in the fun honeymoon stage and still going out and drinking, until I started to get very sick. As in, after every drinking session I would be in fevers for days. Kate was struggling for a couple of days afterwards, too. There is only so much the body can take before it decides to slow down.

While I loved having Kate around, Jäger was unsure, and started to get a bit jealous now that she was taking some of my attention away from him. He would run at her and chest-bump Kate to stamp his authority. One day he got so worked up he started to chase her around the car, then she ran inside and shut the sliding door and he started to bark – which he never did – and chest-bump the door, getting more worked up as he went. He was in no way an aggressive dog but I think just the look of his rough exterior scared people when he came running at you. I was outside and had to raise my voice at him to stop. I then told Kate to get the dog food, because I knew that the way to Jäger's heart was through his stomach. Kate got the bowl of food but was a bit nervous to open the door. Jäger's tune, however, changed in the instant he saw the food. She made him sit and then put down the bowl, made him wait to show she was the boss and then gave him permission to eat. He really made her work for his affection, but since then he has loved her. Phew!

Because if it came down to her or Jäger, I would miss her a lot! He is actually now a Mama's boy and loves to be by her side. She thinks it's because he simply loves her more now, but we both know that it's only because she is the one who feeds him.

Things were going really well between us, and we decided to expand our little family . . . with another dog. While we were in Sydney visiting my dad and I was at an appointment, Kate went shopping to pass the time. She came back not with clothes but with photos of the beagle puppies she had discovered in the mall. Beagles, especially as puppies, have the ability to manipulate anyone into falling in love with them; they just know they are so damned cute! And so our obsession began.

After researching reputable breeders we found an eleven-week-old beagle in the Blue Mountains. I immediately reached out to enquire about him, and the lady responded quickly with a photo of him and a list of his qualities. Kate and I talked it over, and after I assured her that I was a master beagle owner we decided we were definitely going to get him. I rang the breeder to let her know the news and discovered that she was a crazy beagle lady – in a good way – who had raised multiple award-winning beagles and loved them all as her own children, so we knew we were talking to the right person. After putting down a deposit over the phone, we made plans to drive down and pick him up the following week.

I thought this might be a good opportunity to take Kate to Cowra to see her family for a couple of days, then pick up the beagle puppy on the way home. We wanted Jäges to meet the newest member of the family and comfort him on the way back, so we took him along for the road trip. This ten-hour drive to Cowra was going to be the longest trip I had taken since getting my licence back, as well as the longest trip for Jäger. Kate wasn't allowed to drive my car because it was a V8 and she was on her provisional licence, so we planned regular stops along the way for me to stretch out and for Jäges to run around and go to the toilet. We ended up making a stop earlier in the trip than we'd planned, because I was feeling a bit anxious and shaky. When I pulled over I asked Kate how much coffee she had put in my drink.

'Four,' she replied.

I said, 'Four teaspoons?'

'No,' she said, looking confused, 'four tablespoons.'

Well, that explained the buzz! We were by the Port Macquarie turn-off, so we pulled in to take a break. I started to pump myself with bottles of water to try to flush some of the caffeine out of my system. Luckily it was only instant coffee, so the effect doesn't last long. Kate felt horrible and embarrassed, but then after I reassured her that I was okay we were able to laugh about it.

I'm not going to lie: after hearing about the hard times Kate had gone through growing up in Cowra, I wasn't keen on going. We agreed we wouldn't hang out for long.

When we arrived it was freezing – and I mean frozen-bones cold. I'm not a big fan of the cold, and back than I had a really hard time regulating my temperature because of my SCI (spinal-cord injury). Kate wasn't keen on doing too much, so we just hung out with her family for the couple of days we were there. Kate has a really big family, so it was a bit overwhelming to meet them all, but they were all really nice and welcoming. Kate's siblings were all so young then. Her little brother Daimon was three, and it was pretty cool to have him follow me around asking me innocent but personal questions. He watched my every move, and we caught him pretending that he was also in a wheelchair and picking up things the same way I did. It was so cute and also kind of cool that he would want to be like me.

It was a sad goodbye for Kate and her family. Her brother and sisters were heartbroken as we drove away. I hated seeing her so sad about living so far away from her family, but then I reminded her that we had a new boy waiting for us to take him home. We arrived at the breeder's and kept Jäger by the car while we went to meet our new baby. The house was covered in beagle paraphernalia: trophies, pictures, plates, mugs, along with eight actual beagles outside. They were so cute. The breeder brought in our boy and his sister and we watched them run around the house like crazy, tearing everything apart and leaping over furniture. That's how we came to name him Nitro.

We said goodbye to the breeder and introduced Jäges to his new little brother. We let them play for a bit, then before we put them both in the back of the car, we let Nitro say one last goodbye to his sister. That was hard to watch. Within about two minutes of us driving away, Nitro started to howl. We kept driving in the hope he would settle but he kept crying his heartbreaking cry. We looked at each other, wondering if we had done the right thing taking him away from his sister. I pulled over, and Kate moved him to a blanket in the front at her feet, but he continued to cry, and it was only when she lifted him into her arms that, after one last soft howl, he fell asleep on her lap for the rest of the seven-hour drive home. We were so glad he settled, because it would have been the most gut-wrenching trip if he had cried the whole way home.

By the time we got home late that night, Nitro was pretty settled. We put him out in the backyard for the night in the hope he would be fine with Jäger. He whimpered a bit while exploring the yard, that beagle nose going into automatic yard patrol. Jäger must have been pretty scary to a new puppy who had only ever seen his own breed for his whole twelve weeks of life, and after a few howls and some puppy tears, we brought them both into the laundry and set them up a bed in there. It was hard to listen to Nitro cry, but eventually he fell asleep and slept through to the morning.

The next day we played with them both and showed Nitro round the yard and took them for a walk around town. It was a big adjustment for them both, but it didn't take long for the two of them to bond. Jäges's face always looks grumpy by default because he's a bulldog, but we could tell underneath his rough exterior that he was beginning to like having Nitro as his brother, maybe even love him. It was the best thing we could have ever done for Jäger, plus they were the perfect breed match. Jäges is more chilled and happy to just lie around and Nitro is kind of wild and always on the move. They balance each other out perfectly. Jäger liked to let it be known that he was boss, and every time Nitro got a bit out of control or Jäger just wasn't in the mood he would sit on Nitro's big floppy ears. We would often, hear them wrestling at the back door. It was so cute to watch.

* * *

After Kate moved in, she asked if we could get her keyboard out of storage. I knew she enjoyed playing the piano, but little did I know that she could actually *really* play.

One Saturday afternoon I was in my room writing some work emails when I heard music coming from the dining room. It went for bit, then I heard an angelic voice singing along with the music. I thought it was the radio, so I didn't pay much attention, but then in between emails I looked out to see that it was Kate playing the keyboard and singing.

What. The. *Fuck!*

I immediately stopped what I was doing and went out there. 'Wow! You're incredible! Why did you never tell me you're a singer?' I asked as I picked my jaw up off the floor.

'I'm not,' she said with a shy smile.

She proceeded to tell me that she had always wanted to sing but had been too scared to say it out loud. She thought people would just think that she was a dreamer and tell her it wasn't realistic. I asked her to play for me again, and as she sang I really saw her for the first time. Who she was meant to be.

I had never heard a voice like hers, and to top it off she could play the piano and write songs. I remember telling her, 'When you're given a talent like this, you can't hide it, you need to share it with the world.' This was an amazing turning point in our relationship. I believed in her dreams as much as she believed in mine. It was now my mission to help her achieve her dreams, just like she was doing for me.

CHAPTER 14

NEW BEGINNINGS

KADA AND BARNEY

Finally, we can continue our story together. They say that when it comes to matters of the heart, when you know, you know. And so we both knew pretty early on that we had found the love of our lives. It started with sleepovers, to nights away together, to meeting the families, all within the first few months. If we weren't together we were either talking on the phone or texting.

It was a pretty special moment when we exchanged our first I love yous. It was effortless, and as if those three words alone pulled us both out of the darkness and on to the path of greatness.

Falling in love is the easy part. It's easy to become swept up in all the love, locking yourselves away from the real world and all its

Barney was a happy kid, full of energy, with a love for sports, animals and planes, but once he started surfing that was pretty much all he could think about.

Kada's childhood was all about family (*bottom left*) with her three sisters Rachael, Clarissa, Annabelle and brother, Daimon (not pictured), and her imagination. And it was apparent very early that she was a performer, singing at the top of her voice whenever and wherever she could.

For Barney, high school (*below, third from left*) was all about mates and surfing but for Kada, high school was when her troubles began.

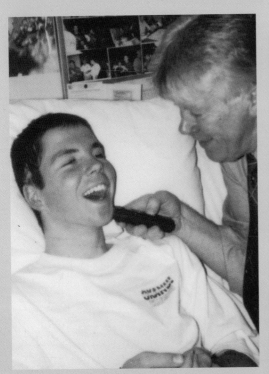

The accident and its aftermath meant big adjustments.
Amongst the trauma, there were some constants – family and friends.

Barney's first surf after the accident was at Pipeline, on the North Shore of Oahu, Hawaii, with Mick Fanning and Adam Penfold.

When Barney met Kada he knew she was the one. Kada felt exactly the same about him.

Kada and Barney with trainer Hayley Reynolds. Rehabilitation and training are part of every day.

left: YES … I couldn't wait to marry my best friend. Thanks Eric and Sachi for helping make this dream-come-true moment happen.

below: Kada and Barney with Nitro and Jäger.

Barney's mum, Helen, has always been his strength.

Our wedding of 'Pure Imagination'. The stars aligned and there was magic in the air that perfect night. *top* with Barney's family and *middle* with Kada's.

bottom left: The premiere of our film, *You and Me*, with Mick Fanning.

bottom right: Bora Bora was the picture-perfect place for our fairytale honeymoon.

Music has always been food for Kada's soul, strengthening her when she feels weak. 'Forever I will live for the music for with it I am free.' – Kada

Jubilation on the beach in California: 2017 Stance ISA World Adaptive Surf Champion of the AS5-Assist division, Barney Miller. Gold for Team Australia!

problems. But the true test of love shines through in how you, as a team, face the challenges thrown at you. This is the time to share your vulnerable side, and in doing so you will see if the relationship is strong enough to break through.

Our first obstacle was to deal with the critics. There were concerns about the eleven-year age gap, and whether a seventeen-year-old was capable of taking on the kind of responsibility required to take care of Barney. Many of those around us were sceptical of the motives behind the relationship and whether it could really work.

KADA

I understand why some people in Barney's life were cautious of me in the beginning. I was so young, had never been in a real relationship and I was committing to one with quite a few extra responsibilities than the average relationship. I would be lying if I said I wasn't hurt or offended, I definitely was. I was offended that they were surprised that someone like me could fall in love with Barney. I think the most hurtful concern was about my motives for moving in with Barney so quickly. The thing was, our relationship was already so strong, and yes I moved in only a few months into it, but it was originally meant to be temporary while I looked for a new place. Rachel was going on holiday and planned to rent out her apartment, so we were both moving out; I was going to move to my cousins' house in Emerald Beach, a forty-minute drive north while I looked. I didn't have my licence, so out of concern that we would never see each other, Barney invited me to stay with him. The new challenge, though, was finding somewhere wheelchair-friendly so Barney could come to my place, but it was more difficult than I'd thought. After talking it through, we decided that I needed to just find a house regardless of its accessibility, but every time I found a potential place, we both found ourselves making excuses for why I couldn't live there. I think we were both scared of the other one thinking it was too soon, but one night while I was scrolling the internet for potential homes, Barney stopped me and gave me his serious face. He asked me if it would be crazy if I just moved in with him. I had already been staying there most nights and it was working out really well. I was a little worried at first but also excited to know that our relationship was heading in the right direction. After a night of talking it over, we agreed that it made the most sense. We certainly got to know each other very intimately, very quickly, but it brought us closer together.

The next challenge came in the form of the third wheel in our relationship: a carer. At that stage Barney had Luke, and although we loved hanging out with him, as a new couple there are times you just want to be alone or go out and do normal couple things. So, we set our first goal together: to do transfers on our own. There was a lot of trial and error, but we both believe that the trick to achieving a goal is to find motivation in the outcome and make your reason for doing it outweigh how hard it is to get there. We were so desperate to gain independence together that we just tried over and over until we got it. To Barney's dismay, it involved me lifting him by the shorts and giving him a wedgie.

BARNEY

I had never been so sure of anything as I was in loving Kate and asking her to move in with me. Sure, it was scary and there were a lot of doubters, but I knew we were meant to be together.

A few months into our relationship, just after Kate had moved in, I had my annual trip to Hawaii planned with the boys. I was going for three weeks, and although it was hard to say goodbye I knew that this was going to be a great opportunity to prove to everyone that we were serious and in it for the long game. Kate was staying at the house by herself with Jäger, but Mum and Mal were across the road if she needed anything. The first couple of nights she brought Jäger inside to keep her company but then on the third night she ended up over the road because she was not comfortable alone in the house. Over the weeks that I was gone she really bonded with my family and they also fell in love with her, which of course was great for me to hear.

Meanwhile in Hawaii, I was having a good time with the boys. One afternoon as I hung out with Mick Fanning we got talking about Kate and I told him how happy I was.

'This is it,' I said. 'It's time and I'm ready. I want to work on myself and I want to walk again.'

I had said this so often before but it was always missing a certain drive behind it. What seemed to motivate me the most was wanting to make things better for the people I care about.

He said to me, 'Well, if you're serious, let's make it happen.' He introduced me to his then trainer Jan Carton, a CHEK-certified health coach. For those who don't know, CHEK stands for Corrective Holistic Exercise Kinesiology, a mind–body approach to healing and exercise. Jan has a world of knowledge and understanding of the human body, and this was my introduction to getting to know mine.

We started with a conversation about my injury, my abilities and my goals. I felt like she was the first person of a professional status to see me for all I could be. She assessed my mobility and sensation with small cues. Before talking to her, I was very slumped in my chair, barely able to move my arms above my waist without losing balance. After a short session of slight movement and breathing exercises, she had me sitting upright in my chair with almost perfect posture for the first time since my accident.

A wave of emotion flooded through me. I was happy, but I was also angry. Why hadn't I been doing this the whole time? Why had nobody shown me that I could do this? It was overwhelming, but I remember Jan came and put her hands on either shoulder facing me and looked into my eyes. She said, 'Whatever you are feeling about the past, it doesn't matter. What matters now is that you know you have the ability to improve and to heal. That was just a small taste of what's to come for you. Greatness is in you, it's your job to let it shine through.'

I immediately felt better and more motivated than ever. This time was different, this time I had a reason bigger than myself: I wanted to give Kate a life that made her proud to be with me.

After three weeks away I returned home to my girl. She came to the airport with my parents to pick me up and as I kissed her hello she said, 'Don't ever leave me for that long ever again, I missed you.'

We spent hours talking about the trip. I told her about Jan and my new goals, and to hear how supportive she was just made it feel even more right. This is where our epic journey together began.

KADA

Summer was a string of parties, and we drank a lot. For me, I was the new girl in town and the new girl in Barney's life. I wanted his friends to like me, plus I was a lot younger than most of them and so I guess I tried to keep up with them. I think I also found comfort in drinking to make up for the age difference but also to give me confidence to talk to them. I felt very intimidated because they all had so much history together and I didn't really know if we would have anything in common. But then something strange started to happen. For two people who could drink and back it up day in and day out, we both started to suffer from chronic hangovers. Barney's would lead to days of fever, from shivering to sweats, and mine came in the form of vomiting all day and into the night. It was coming to the end of summer, I had just turned eighteen and instead of my drinking days beginning they were coming to an end. After Barney's fever broke for the third time we had a long discussion about our lives. We had talked so much about wanting to be better but we hadn't been putting that into practice. So, we decided to make a change together. We didn't say we wouldn't ever drink again, but we started to fill our weekends with dinners and movies instead of booze. Barney called Jan Carton and made an appointment for us to go up to the Gold Coast and start this new program, and I just knew in my gut that things were about to get a lot better for us.

* * *

When I met Jan for the first time at the CHEK Institute on the Gold Coast she was so present, and spoke so certainly of her belief in the human body's ability to heal and regenerate when given the right environment and support, that I felt instantly safe. She explained the basis of kinesiology to us and the methods of mind–body connection. Nothing can really work in sync until you can make that connection. I was intrigued; it sparked something in me that I had never experienced before: a thirst to know more. I wanted Barney to have as much to work with as possible and Jan opened up my mind to a whole new world of possibilities. She helped us understand that we are more than what we see.

BARNEY

Jan was the first person to say to me, 'If you want to be out of the chair you need to train out of the chair.' She had me on the floor assisting me through commando crawls, on the wall sitting right up against it doing snow-angel arms. In just one session I was doing arm movements that I hadn't been able to do in eight years. The sessions were three hours long over four consecutive days. Every day I regained something new: a twitch of a muscle, a posture hold, a hand squeeze. These were all huge milestones for me. I had never done anything like this type of work before, and I was a whole new level of exhausted, both physically and mentally.

KADA

After four mind-blowing days with Jan, she recommended we purchase some equipment to help Barney continue his workouts. We drove to Workout World and Barney waited in the car while I went into the store. A lovely sales guy came out to the car to talk over options with Barney, and after we explained to him that Barney was a quadriplegic he told us about a customer who also had a spinal injury and had just come home from a rehab centre in California. He told us they had this man walking in a walker over there, and he took our number and gave us his customer's number in case we were interested in making contact.

BARNEY

There were so many questions. Was it stem cell? Was it robotic mechanics? I wasn't interested in trying anything invasive, and the many stories of different treatments were all a bit overwhelming. So, I let myself stop thinking about it for a while, until a few weeks later when I received a phone call from a guy named Paul Bailey – he was a paraplegic from the Gold Coast who had just been to America for treatment. Workout World gave him my number and he called to tell me that if I wanted to walk, then I needed to go. The facility he spoke of was Project Walk, a spinal-injury recovery centre. The following week we drove up to the Gold Coast to meet Paul and hear his story. He was so passionate about the treatment and told us of many clients with my injury who had been making life-changing improvements. Was this it? we wondered. Had we just found the gold mine that I had been waiting for?

KADA

I started on a research frenzy. I devoured every word, watched every testimonial video and learnt everything I could about the centre. It was located in Carlsbad, near San Diego in California. This was it, we thought. This was really it. We were overwhelmed by emotion – mostly excitement – but we decided to keep the information to ourselves until we figured out all the logistics. We had to set out our budget to cover airline tickets for us both, nursing services, accessible accommodation, a car and then the treatment. We already had a trip to South Africa booked for July that year, and we wanted to go in summer, so we decided to book in for a three-month block for the summer of 2009.

We had just over a year to plan out every detail and save money. To help budget I decided to take on the role as Barney's carer, that way we didn't need to pay for someone else to travel with us. I also worked at Supré in the Park Beach Plaza part time so I could help save every dollar towards the trip. When we shared our plan with Barney's family they were excited for us but also a little sceptical. We got the same reaction from a lot of our friends. We totally understood their concerns – they didn't want us to get our hopes up and come home disappointed – but we knew it wasn't going to be a miracle quick-fix three months that would send him home walking. What we did know, though, was that at worst it would be an experience for us as a couple, living together in another country, and Barney would be stronger than when he left. For us, that was why we chose to go ahead with it, and also I don't think we could have lived with the thought of what if, if he didn't at least try.

BARNEY

Was I scared? Yes, of course I was. I needed it to be what I was hoping it would be, but it almost seemed too good to be true. I had dealt with enough hard times, though, that I was ready to make something good happen, for my family and friends who had stuck by me, for Kate who believed in me, and for myself.

KADA

South Africa was my first trip overseas, and it changed me. It was Barney, Toby and me, and then we met up with Mick Fanning and the boys from the tour. My eyes were open to what it really meant to not only survive but also live a life filled with love and passion. The people we met in South Africa seemed to truly live and they make their own fun. I remember Barney's nurse Sandy telling us a story about her days of working in the missions. She told me of the kids playing with a cardboard box, some sticks and rocks and someone running around with a plastic bag. They had created a game of pool. That story stuck with me, it taught me that it really doesn't matter where you are or what you have; if you can trust and allow your own imagination to shine through, you can be happy.

BARNEY

The annual trip to Hawaii was here again, and this time – 2008 – Kate came. She loved South Africa but she had dreamt of visiting Hawaii her whole life, so it was pretty special to have her come along and see the place that also gave me so much hope. A lot of my big decisions have been made in Hawaii: deciding to get back in the water, then to surf, to meeting Jan and deciding to dedicate myself to learning to walk again. There must be something in the water that just helps me find the answers I deep down already know. One of these answers came to us one night at the Rip Curl house during a party for one of the local boys who had qualified for the tour. We ran into our friend Taylor Knox, who lives in Carlsbad; he was stoked to hear that we were coming the next summer, and he introduced us to his trainer, Paul Hiniker, who was also from Carlsbad (he even had it tattooed on his rock-solid abs). We spent hours talking about the program, and he told me that he was also a certified CHEK practitioner, and at the end of the conversation he offered for Kate and me to stay with him. He had a two-storey house with a bedroom downstairs and it was just him and his son,

Cannon. We were so grateful for the offer and thanked him but we thought it was probably more courtesy than a real offer. The following day, however, while everyone nursed their hangovers, Paul came over to tell me again that he was serious about the offer. I remember telling him I thought that it was just drunk talk – only to then learn that he doesn't drink. Of course he doesn't, he is the world's fittest man. He gave me his number and email and told us that he would really love to have us come stay. We gratefully accepted, and couldn't help but think that maybe it was all meant to be.

KADA

Hawaii was everything and more than I hoped it would be. It is a magical place that just feels right. I think my Polynesian roots come alive when I'm on an island. This tropical paradise definitely holds a special place in my heart. I have been blessed to have been back four times now and Barney nine. Every time it energises our souls and gives us a new outlook on life.

The stars were aligning for us, leading us onto the path to creating a better life for ourselves. I never knew how much going on Barney's journey was going to also help me and change my life. It has been the greatest gift of all.

CHAPTER 15

CALIFORNIA DREAMING

KADA AND BARNEY

Some of our greatest experiences have come from taking a leap of faith. We have learnt that even through tragedy, there is a beautiful plan waiting on the other side and sometimes we simply need to close our eyes and trust that it will all work out. Barney was ten years post-injury and this next chapter was the beginning of our beautiful plan coming to life.

KADA

There were a few tears as we said goodbye to our family, friends, dogs and Sawtell. The immediate future was unknown but the adventure that awaited us was exciting. We made a pact to enjoy it all no matter the outcome.

I had already lived away from my family, but this was Barney's first real stint away from his family for such a long period of time. For the next three months he had just me and I had just him. We were each other's support.

I was excited to learn that we were only an hour south of Disneyland. America had been a dream of mine since I was a little girl. A friend we had met in South Africa, Cassandra, was kind enough to pick us up from the airport and drive us down to Carlsbad. We arrived at our new home in the late afternoon, where Paul was waiting to welcome us and introduce us to his ten-year-old son, Cannon.

I love when you can pinpoint the exact moment that triggered a different, lifelong choice. Living with Paul was kind of a wake-up call to our eating habits. Because he was very healthy it felt disrespectful to bring unhealthy food into the house, so by default we started to make healthier choices. Paul would teach me how to cook different meals and was always happy to give me health and exercise tips.

Apart from our diet, there were many adjustments needed to make this all work. Barney couldn't get into the shower at Paul's house, so we adopted the outside-shower – under the hose with a bucket of hot water – method. The thing we were not banking on, though, was for it to be the coldest summer California had had in years. There is a fog that comes over every day called a marine layer. It's where the hot air from the desert meets the cold air of the ocean and it's quite confusing if you have no idea what it is; you simply think it's an overcast day. Those days were tough for poor Barney, but he was a trooper. We had made the decision to save the money on hiring a nursing service and put it towards our living expenses and I would become Barney's nurse. For the months leading up to our trip I had the community nurses and morning nurses training me on everything from changing his catheter to bathroom routines. I thought I would be overwhelmed by it all but surprisingly it felt very natural. My next task was driving on the other side of the road. I had barely driven on the empty roads of Australia and I was about to take on Californian traffic in all its glory. When I pulled out of the car-rental parking lot, I immediately froze. But I quickly recalled the memo I had come up with to help me remember what side to stay on: drivers are always on the inside of the road. The car's odometer is also in miles not kilometres, so getting used to what that meant was a whole other thing. I remember the first day driving: Barney wanted to check the surf, so he directed me straight onto the freeway. I totally freaked out and drove forty miles an hour, but very quickly realised that if I didn't keep up with the traffic I would cause an accident from going too slow. A few days on the road, though, and I was well adjusted to the fast pace of California.

* * *

As soon as we walked through the doors of Project Walk we felt welcomed with positive energy. Everyone is there for the same reason: to improve their ability. There were clients with every level injury at every different stage in the recovery. New clients starting out like us, to ones who had been there since Project Walk opened. Some who were learning to move their arms, some learning to roll over, and some even taking their first steps. It was simply empowering to know that we were definitely in the right place.

BARNEY

I knew there was no quick fix but I was also excited to see what my body could accomplish in the next three months. My initial consultation was with Jason Smith. Jason had a background in body building and from first impressions he had a hard-arse personality to match. His first question to me was: 'Okay, I see you're ten years post-injury – what are your goals?' I answered: 'Well, what everyone else wants: I want to walk.' He looked back over my paperwork and suggested we set some smaller goals to start, such as transfers and rolling over. Initially I was a little disheartened, but I decided to take it as a challenge to break him, to one day hear Jason tell me that I *will* walk.

Project Walk would never give anyone false hope, they wouldn't mention walking until they were sure that was the direction a client was heading. It is a lot of hard work and dedication, and I was ten years post-injury, which made me the longest post-injury patient they had ever seen. I was really starting from the ground up because I was the typical statistic of a quadriplegic then. I had no movement at all in my lower limbs except for the uncontrolled spasms I would get pulsing through my legs. I had a few positive things going for me, though. I hadn't lost any bone density over the ten-year period. The lady doing my scans even did them twice because she thought there must have been a mistake. I also had taken myself off Baclofen, the muscle-relaxant drug that most patients with an SCI are prescribed to help relieve their spasms. I always saw spasms as a good thing; even though they hurt like a cramp and I couldn't control them, I welcomed them as movement and circulation for my legs. And I also believe that this kept my legs in good condition for all those years while they were asleep. Patients with an SCI are usually told if you don't regain any movement after two years, then you never will. This can be a daunting diagnosis and one that seals a lot of patients' fates. Thankfully this was one moment where my stubbornness worked well in my favour. I don't give up without a fight. Even a long ten-year battle.

If I wanted to move on to each new phase, I needed to get stronger. So, we began with the task of self-transferring. They told me to visualise pushing through my feet in order to gain more strength to lift across, and it made me realise how often I had mindlessly neglected my legs. It's amazing how powerful those small cues are at targeting specific muscles. It didn't take me very long to master the self-transfer. Jason was a great motivator because he wouldn't help me unless I was falling; it became a survivor-style scenario and one I was determined to beat.

I remember arriving one day to hear Jason ask if I could sit up from lying on my back. He wasn't interested in how I did it, just if I could. Before I knew it I was saying yes, determined to show him. The truth was, I had never done it, so I went for the fake-it-till-you-make-it strategy. I wanted to prove to him that I was capable of more than the tasks he had been giving me. It must have been something about not wanting to admit that I couldn't do it that somehow allowed me to pull it off. I started by rolling over, and then hustled my way up with my elbows. It was actually a lot easier than I thought it would be, and again another stream of thoughts started to run through my mind, berating me for not having tried any of this before. None of that mattered, though. What did matter was that I had surprised even myself with my own ability. What else could I do that I had never tried?

Over the following weeks I learnt to bridge with hip extension and glute activation, meaning I could lift my hips in the air while lying on my back with feet planted on the ground. This was a huge milestone and a new sign of how well my body was responding to the therapy. Project Walk used an exercise kinesiology–based method to help stimulate the mind–body connection. They were pretty much taking me back to a baby stage and taking me through all the motor skills again. They worked with the spasms to help turn them into controlled movement patterns.

After I began to master bridging, Jason realised I was there for the long haul and I wasn't afraid to try anything he threw at me. A typical session would start on the table doing stretches and range-of-movement sequencing to warm up my body for the next hour of core stabilising and controlled movement, which was usually done in a kneeling position or on the floor. The third hour would be the advanced part of the session, focusing and enhancing my movement and strength. I loved being up in the standing frame. It was nice to be able to look down into Kate's eyes for the first time. We would even dance together, which made us both laugh.

I did have my limitations, though. I was desperate to feel that walking pattern again and I wanted to try the motorised treadmill, but my body wasn't quite ready yet. However I was even more determined than ever to keep going and never give up.

* * *

Carlsbad is home to some of the world's best action-sport athletes. It's a mega hub for surfers and has some great surf spots up and down the coast. I had met a kid named Patrick at

Project Walk. He was around fifteen years old and he loved to surf. He was run over by a reversing car when he was eighteen months old and had grown up in his wheelchair. He never let it stop him from pursuing the things he wanted, though. He told me about surf days hosted by an organisation called Wheels to Water. They were designed to get people with limited movement out in the water and catching as many waves as possible. So, I signed up. The founder, Travis, was an awesome guy with a big heart. He didn't do it for the recognition, he just loved surfing and wanted to share the experience with others who otherwise wouldn't get to do it. They hosted an event once a month up and down the coast from Newport Beach down to La Jolla Shores.

The one thing I didn't count on was how cold the water temperature actually was. It turns out, *Baywatch* lied to us. They could not have been swimming in that water. It was colder than our winter water back home. In fact, the Californian summer that we had been sold in movies was not quite as summery as we expected. We didn't pack any warm clothes at all, and we regretted it.

Wheels to Water finished up after a few summers. I was so grateful to all the volunteers, especially Travis, for giving me that outlet and opportunity in those first few years. Surfing is so healing, and it probably sounds crazy but I love a good wipeout. It loosens my whole body up like a good natural adjustment from the ocean. We also noticed that on the weeks that I surfed, my body responded better to training. So, surfing was helping my training? Well, I needed no excuse to surf more, but now having a reason to up it and get out there more was a surprising bonus.

KADA

One thing we have both always loved and found natural is making friends, and we were so grateful to be able to do this in California. Barney was training Mondays, Tuesdays, Thursdays and Fridays for three hours a day. On his days off we would often explore the wonders of California; there was so much to see in three months. Through Taylor and Paul we started to make some new friends. Taylor's now wife, Ann-Marie, became a close friend who helped make the transition a lot easier. Tim Fox was another one; he became one of Barney's surf buddies, always up for helping out. Some friends from home, Kingy and Nadene, were also living in Malibu at the time. When another friend, Griggsy, visited from home he stayed with Taylor and Ann-Marie, and Kingy and Nadene came down to visit. I had just bought myself a piano, and after dinner we all went back to Paul's and I played for everyone. I hadn't performed in public for years but somehow it felt time to let my voice out again. It was in their eyes and response that really told me that this is what I should be doing with my life. I had been so scared for so long to admit it out loud, that I didn't even know how to say it.

But there I was, living in California with my boyfriend who was doing intense rehabilitation to learn to do what science and statistics said was impossible, so what was there to be scared of? Nothing.

The following Thursday I signed up for an open-mic night at the Hill Street Cafe in Oceanside. I knew that if I could master my performance there and captivate an intimate audience, then I could perform anywhere. And that's exactly what I did. Our Thursday nights became open-mic nights, and week after week I sang to strangers and friends, each time hearing the same words, 'You were born for this.' The more I heard it, the more I began to believe it. It felt good; no, it felt great to share my gift with others. I cannot thank Taylor, Ann-Marie, Griggsy, Tim, Paul, Kingy and Nadene, and of course my best friend, Barney, for giving me the courage to chase this dream. I took a leap into the unknown that night when I sang to them in Paul's living room and when they all responded with love and support and encouragement it allowed me to see myself as more than I had ever seen myself before. A singer.

Three months came to an end and we had made such a positive change and taken a huge step forward in our life together. We were booked to return to Project Walk the following year at the same time. We were sad to leave but excited to get home to our dogs and friends and family. We couldn't wait to share all our experiences with everyone and show them the improvements that Barney had made.

We had fitted so much into our time there. We visited Disneyland (which really is the happiest place on earth), Hollywood, San Diego Zoo and SeaWorld (which left us heartbroken for the orcas). We surfed, we developed a love of Mexican food and we made some pretty awesome new friends. Oh, and we even went to a few concerts like Snoop Dogg, Poison and Mötley Crüe – tickets were $25–30. Mindblowing.

The hardest part about going home was knowing we would not have the same consistent workout program that Barney had stuck to for the previous three months, nor access to the same type of training. We tried to replicate as much as we could on our own but it was definitely hard. The most important thing was to keep Barney's body as active as possible. This meant keeping his legs constantly stimulated and moving.

Those three months taught us a lot about ourselves and our relationship. Spending so much time together brought us even closer even though at times we wanted to strangle each other. We learnt that our strength together lies within us believing in each other's dreams. It is the very core of what our relationship is built on and what makes us work so well together. Above all, we will never give up on each other.

CHAPTER 16

STANDING ON TOP OF THE WORLD

KADA AND BARNEY

Life had catapulted us in a new direction, a journey we were both happy to be on. Our life in many ways is very unconventional. We dance to our own beat and make up the rules as we go, but we also don't really like rules because they often limit an outcome based on what we think we should do rather than what we feel. We still had a lot of demons to face and insecurities to overcome but one thing we could always count on was each other.

KADA

It was so nice to be home in Sawtell with all of our friends and family. Skype had made it easier to keep in contact with everyone while we were travelling, but as much as we'd tried to attract the attention of our dogs to the camera they weren't really into it. So, it was good to have their slobbery kisses back in our lives.

We definitely have the best of both worlds when it comes to living in Sawtell. It's insanely beautiful. It has small-town charm with access to a larger city only ten minutes away. It's a conveniently close drive to Byron Bay or the Gold Coast, which are regular getaways for us. We also have the added benefit of the airport if things get a little too quiet for us and we are ready to jet off somewhere else for some added adventure. I have always had a nomadic drive within me. There is something so soul-satisfying about living a spontaneous lifestyle. One of the many things that has made our relationship so good is our ever-changing life. No week is ever really the same for us. We decided pretty early on in our relationship to always be open to opportunity and say yes to adventure. My parents found this very surprising given throughout my childhood I suffered from chronic travel sickness. Even travelling to my grandmother's farm ten minutes out of town made me sick, and school trips always had me at the front of the bus with a sick bucket no matter how hard I tried to pretend that I was okay. Back then even the mention of travel would make me gag, but I never let it stop me from going anywhere because the adventure waiting for me on the other side of it always made it totally worth it.

We tried everything to avoid it: chewing gum, ginger chews, car-sickness wristbands, bandaids over the belly button – nothing ever worked. We just hoped that one day I would grow out of it. My mum got pretty efficient at emptying the bucket on the side of the road.

Fast-forward to meeting Barney and my life being thrown into a completely new territory of never-ending road trips, and somehow it stopped. It was a whole new experience to go on a road trip without being sick. Almost a new lease on life, like I had been released from a horrible curse and I had a chance to start over. And that I did. Road trips are a safe haven for me now. I find a lot of inspiration while mindlessly driving and listening to the soundtracks of our childhoods. Also finding that independence as a couple to even go on road trips by ourselves was a feat in itself. I think that's what makes it even more special. It really speaks volumes of truth that if you want something, you have to go out and get it.

My relationship with my parents had really transformed into a rock-solid bond. I spoke with my mum most days, and the plan was always for them to eventually move to Coffs Harbour, they just weren't sure when that would happen. They originally told me five years, although they hoped for earlier. The rest of my family also started talking about moving closer to us. It started with my Aunty Jess and Uncle Nathan, when Nathan was offered a new job in Coffs. I was ecstatic. I couldn't believe that I was finally going to have some family around after only two years. Then my Aunty Naomi called me to tell me she had a new job at a local school. I couldn't believe what was happening. Naomi and Brett had lived in Wollongong for the previous five years, so it was a real surprise to have them coming to live close by. Then I got the call. Not only were my mum and dad and siblings moving up in the coming months, but so were my Aunty Bernice and Uncle Andrew and their kids and my nanno and grandad. I had never known that the rest of them also had the intention of moving, though I did often say how great it would be if they all moved so I could spend Christmas with both Barney's family and mine every year. Maybe my words had more power than I realised?

On 4 January 2010, the entire family arrived in town. We had arranged for my parents and siblings to move in with us while they looked for a place and also to housesit and look after the dogs for us when we went back to California. They moved in upstairs and we shared the kitchen and laundry. I was so excited to finally have them there. Rachael, Clarissa and Annabelle were enrolled in school, but because Daimon was only four he got to stay home and hang out with us on the days he wasn't in pre-school.

I was so happy, and it was an added bonus to have Mama Bear in the house to cook and teach me recipes and also occasionally do our washing. It was nice to get a second-do over at living with them, but this time round I was grateful to have them and be part of the family. It was also nice that Barney was now part of the family too. Every morning I would do exercises and stretches with Barney, and Annabelle and Daimon would come in to help. Belle always kept count to make sure that none of us were skipping short, well, mainly me.

BARNEY

The months rolled by and before we knew it we were back in California for my next round of training. The flights always take it out of me, so it took a few weeks to get back in the swing of things but not as long as I thought it might. It was hard adjusting after being home for the previous eight months without the same intensity in my training program. Kate and I had tried to train together as much as we could but because my body was still pretty weak there was only so much that we could do together. We were fortunate to be staying with Paul again for the summer. This time round the transition of settling in to the fast-paced lifestyle wasn't as daunting and we had really begun to find our bearings in what we were hoping would become our home away from home.

Training was starting to ramp up, I was back working with Jason and this time he had a new trainer shadowing him through some sessions. His name was Josh and little did I know that he would come to be my master trainer but also one of my best mates. The previous trip had gone really well in terms of my training, so at first I put a lot of pressure on myself about what I was doing then compared to where I was now. I was also really impatient and spent a lot of time wanting to be at the next stage already. I was so consumed by my goal that I had forgotten the most important thing of all: to enjoy the journey. The journey was and should be just as important as the end goal – these were words that Arthur Pascoe had said to me years earlier and they were finally beginning to make sense. The moment I took that on board and let go of all of the stress that I had wound around it all, was when the improvements really began.

Project Walk was starting to get busier and my sessions were starting to shift between trainers. I was placed with a trainer named Mica, who was small but a firecracker. To this day, Mica is still one of the toughest, most amazing trainers I have had the pleasure of working with. After my first session with her I immediately went to the front office to request more hours with her. The combo I had going with Jason/Josh and Mica was working really well. Then Eric, the co-founder and head of research, was thrown into the mix and I suddenly had a dream team. They each had their own spin on techniques, and what I loved about them all was that they weren't afraid to step out of the box and experiment with different set-ups. Each client's program was very specific to their injury and their capabilities, and mine grew and changed depending on what my body was doing and responding to. Mica had an awesome way of explaining what she was doing and what she was looking for from me, and then being able to exploit that until she got the response she was looking for from the muscle. Working with her also taught me the importance of building a strong foundation. I had been so fixated on wanting to try all the fancy cool equipment that I didn't realise that none of it mattered unless I could stabilise through my core, which I couldn't until she literally woke it up. It wasn't uncommon for me to be covered in bruises after she had finished poking and prodding me for activation pressure points. But I wouldn't have had it any other way.

KADA

I had asked our friend Mick Fanning for advice on pursuing your passion as a career, and told him that I wanted to chase my music dream. He was so encouraging and put me in contact with a friend of his named Kevin Zinger who owned a record label in LA. His label wasn't really suited to me and what I was doing but he opened up his schedule for a dinner to meet and chat about music. He had a place in Carlsbad where he often spent the weekend, so on his next trip down we met at Vigilucci's in downtown Carlsbad. I hadn't even seen a picture of him, so we had no idea what to expect. I made Barney wear a nice shirt and pants and no hat. (Anyone who knows Barney knows that it's a rare sight to see him not wearing his beloved hat.) We arrived and the maître d' directed us to our table to meet Zinger and his friend, there he was in denim shorts, a denim vest and T-shirt and a baseball cap. Barney looked at me in disgust and whispered, 'I look like a dickhead.'

We got talking about the music I love, my influences and where I wanted to take it. I told him that there is a place for every type of music in my life but my influences were Alicia Keys, Mariah Carey, Jewel, Nelly Furtado, Destiny's Child and Whitney. If you were to ask me now, it would still be pretty much the same but the list has also grown a lot. That's the magical thing about music, it's forever changing and there is inspiration in everything.

Kevin connected me with a producer close by, and I worked with them for a year on a few tracks. It was exciting to be in a studio environment and an experience I will forever be grateful for. Already, my childhood dream of moving to California and recording my music had come true. To be honest, though, my songwriting was nowhere near as developed as I needed it to be.

The night before the fourth of July we were invited to a barbecue at a friend's house. Paul asked me to bring my keyboard to perform for them. After everyone ate I set up the keyboard and played for the intimate group of five people. I was a little nervous, but as soon as I started to sing, again it just felt natural. There is something so magical that happens when I sing in public. It's like my heart steps forward and is singing with me. After I finished I got chatting to a friend of Paul's, Jason, who was a sports agent. We talked about my direction and I told him that I was ready to give it a shot and pursue music as a career. I think back now on how much I really wanted it. I used to carry the keyboard in the back of the car for any given moment to whip it out and perform on demand. It actually makes me wonder why I still don't do that. You just never really know who is ready to listen and what opportunities it will lead you to. Jason asked if I would be interested to see what he could do to help build my brand. Music wasn't his industry but I was grateful that he wanted to help, so we shook hands and got to work making a game plan.

Jason invited us to his place for fourth of July celebrations, and as we arrived another friend of ours happened to walk past and invited us to a party a few houses down the road. We decided to all head to the party down the road, where we met some fellow Aussies. These included a music duo, their manager and a friend of theirs Scott – who we later became close friends with and who was travelling with them. The boys were performing, and after their set, Jason – my 'manager' for all of twenty minutes – told everyone about my musical abilities and they all insisted I get my keyboard out and play too. I couldn't help but laugh about the way opportunities just crop up sometimes, and we have to make the most of them.

BARNEY

Training had been amazing, and I was making small progressions day by day. Jason, my trainer, threw at me the idea to try to free-stand. Of course I was game, I was game to try anything when it came to my training. I am not one to back down from a challenge; besides, what's there to be scared of? I had already broken my neck. I had fallen more times than I could count, so there was really no reason to be scared of trying an exercise that may or may not work. Even if it didn't work out the first or the tenth time I wasn't afraid to keep trying till it did and then again until it became natural. This is what happened on the road to standing. It all started with Jason taking me through a series of leg movements and sit-ups to activate my core, then stomps to ground out my feet. He would then sit me on the edge of a table and push down through my shoulders to fire up my abs again, then rock me back and in one swift motion pull me up onto my feet. Josh or Kate would often be behind ready to push my hips and glutes through. Jason had the vision that I was close to getting it because my hip-flex bridging was so powerful. If you still don't know what I'm talking about, imagine me doing a big power thrust on my back. Classic Thunder From Down Under. They began to get me standing up against a ballet-style bar with my hands strapped in, straightening my legs and locking out my knees with boxes in front for safety, while they held my hips in position. It felt so good to be upright more often and a step closer to standing with Kate. We were able to take our first photo together standing side by side.

KADA

I have always been a bit of a dreamer. One of my favourite conversation subjects is always Imagine If This Happened. The most amazing thing about this game is that more than half the things I say actually eventually happen. My mum told Barney pretty early on in our relationship: be careful what she wishes for, it always comes true. For a long time I put it down to coincidence or just plain luck, but after it kept happening too many times to ignore I started to wonder what it was. Of course for a second I thought maybe I am a mythical being with a supernatural ability or maybe I am making these things happen unintentionally. There have been a string of events that I will tell you about throughout the next few chapters that really changed the way I live my life and how I direct my thoughts.

The first incident that had me believing in destiny or even us creating our own destiny was the moment I realised that Barney was in the car accident with the boy whose family went to my church growing up. I had prayed when I was just nine years old that Barney would survive and go on to live a happy life having never met him or even knowing who he was – and here we are living the best life together. It was the first time in my life that I had heard of someone close to my world being in an accident and who needed prayer. I had this automatic empathic emotion that takes over and felt so connected with the desire to do something to help, so when I said my prayer that day, I meant it with every part of me. I can't help but believe that it was more than just a prayer, it was a destiny.

Sometimes I go through manic episodes of life planning: I will get an idea in my head and then roll with it and then I also create an entire scenario down to every fine detail. As an example, our friend Corey is a professional BMX rider, and we had planned a trip with friends to watch him compete in the X Games in LA. It suddenly occurred to me that Corey and Carey Hart were friends and that Carey was also going to be at the X Games. So, just like that the ideal plan started to form in my mind: *Well, if Carey is there, of course P!nk will be there to support him, OMG I'm going to meet P!nk today!*

Honestly, sometimes Barney thinks I'm actually crazy with the ideas that pop into my head but I swear there is always logic to my momentary lapses of sanity.

We arrived at our first-ever X Games, which was such a different scene from the surfing contests yet at the same time it shared the same vibe. The day went by and I had actually forgotten that I didn't see Carey or meet P!nk but when we got in the car, Barney reminded me. I'm not going to lie, I was a little bummed because that was the perfect scenario in my head, but I also accepted that life doesn't always work out the way you plan it, no matter how much effort and detail you put into it.

The following weekend we were invited to the premiere of the surf film of another friend, Julian, in Costa Mesa. We almost weren't going to go because it was an hour's drive away but then at the last minute we agreed we needed to show our support, so we booked a hotel room and drove up for a night out. There were people everywhere at the premiere, and as we waited for our friend Hicksy to bring our drinks from the bar, another friend Taz pulled me in close and whispered, 'Don't freak out, but casually look up to the balcony.' You know when someone says 'casually look' or 'don't look now', what do you do? Immediately turn around. I looked up, and there before my eyes were Carey Hart and P!nk. I almost died. Hicksy came back with our drinks and asked what all the excitement was about, and when I told him, he oh-so-casually said to me, 'Oh, I know Carey. Want me to introduce you?' I actually choked on my drink as he said it. Mind you, he was also pretty drunk, so I wasn't sure whether to get my hopes up, so I said, 'Well, obviously yes, but no pressure,' though a part of me was extremely anxious at the thought of actually talking to her. She is, after all, the pinnacle of women's empowerment in the music industry and the very standard of what a true performer should be.

We made our way up to the VIP lounge on the top balcony and the butterflies were high. I am not really one to get star-struck, but P!nk is one person who I just adore and after I saw her in concert a few years earlier she made it to the top of my bucket list of people to meet. We walked into the gated-off area and over to where she and Carey were standing. Hicksy made the intro and she graciously hugged me and said, 'Hi, I'm Alecia.'

I was lost for words. She was so beautiful and more than I could have even imagined. We posed for a picture and when Hicksy gave me back the camera it was blurry but I didn't want to hassle them for another one, but she grabbed the camera from me to check it and instantly demanded a better one. Thank God because that would have been so disappointing. We took a few more and she gave her nod of approval. I thanked her for the photos but also for being such an incredible role model in music. I wish I'd had the courage back then to tell her my aspirations but I didn't. Maybe soon it won't matter because I will be singing alongside her in the charts and one day I can tell her again in person how much that moment meant to me.

So, was it a coincidence that I had made a master plan to meet P!nk and although it didn't happen how I had planned it, it still happened and it was perfect? Maybe it was, but I honestly don't think so. If this was just a one-time incident I totally would have written it off as a crazy cool thing that happened to me, but I have experienced in so many ways that nothing is in fact random, there is purpose to everything that happens and we have more influence over it than most of us realise.

BARNEY

It was towards the end of our second consecutive three-month trip that it happened. Again we stayed with Paul and Cannon, and again it was so much fun. We would look after Cannon whenever Paul had an overnight trip away and were so happy to because Cannon was such a cool kid and was super cruisy. We also wanted to help Paul out because he had been such an amazing friend letting us stay with him while we were over there. I know he enjoyed us staying, too, but as good as this was, we knew we couldn't depend on doing this forever – and we planned to come back year after year. Even when I was back on my feet full-time we would return because it is such an amazing place where we have made so many friends who felt like family, so it was starting to feel like our second home.

Just out of interest I started to look at property prices in the North County; it's something I like doing wherever we go in the world. The house market in America had crashed severely, so houses weren't nearly as expensive as I'd expected. We looked at a few places online and then drove past them to see what they really looked like and to check out the accessibility;

we figured – in a vague, non-committed way – that if we did look into buying one, we could rent it out to other people who were visiting for therapy with their families. We very quickly found that a lot of complexes to rent or buy in the areas we were looking didn't have very good accessibility. They all either had stairs going in and out of the property or were double-storey townhouses.

After a few weeks of trawling the internet we decided to contact a real-estate agent so we could look inside a couple of the places. It was fun just killing time as well. We contacted Dennis and Donna Smolinski, and little did we know at the time the role they would come to play in our lives. Dennis and Donna were an older couple in their early seventies who mainly bought foreclosed houses super cheap to then do them up and sell them off, but they were more than happy to show two young Aussies into a few houses for a bit of fun as well.

Dennis was a tall, thin, white-haired groover with a deep love of bright Tommy Bahama shirts, although on occasion he would be dressed in a full Adidas tracksuit with boat shoes. This man had style. Donna was a hard-driven business woman who looked as though she spent much of her time keeping Dennis in check because he was really passionate and would get over-excited about many things.

When we first met, after they had prepared a list of properties to show us, Dennis said one of the funniest but most sincere things anyone has ever said to me. 'Listen Barney,' he said, 'we've spoken a lot over the past couple of days and I like you! I'm seventy-two and I haven't got many more years left on this planet, and you seem like a real driven person in your goal of walking. So, you need six guys to carry a coffin and I've only got five mates I'd actually trust and I want you to be that sixth person to carry me in the coffin when I go.'

I didn't know what to say so I laughed a bit and then realised he was actually serious. I then replied, 'I would be honoured!'

We looked through a few properties that day but none met all our requirements. A lot of places had separate communal parking lots away from the residence, or steps going in or out. The more Dennis found, the less chance we thought it would happen, if we ever decided to seriously look into buying one. But then he came upon a place that looked right: three bedrooms, two bathrooms, a lock-up double garage and a private courtyard you could walk through from the garage to the condo. And, it was all one level, which was rare in the area. It had been a recent foreclosure and an investors' group had purchased it and renovated the interior. Brand-new thick carpet was laid throughout the entire condo except for the kitchen and bathrooms. We laughed saying, 'Well, this carpet will be the first to go. It's like pushing through sand.' We loved the place, though, it was perfect. It was close to the shops, training and only a ten-minute drive to the beach.

Dennis asked what we'd like to do, and after Kate and I talked about it that night we decided we could throw out an offer much lower than the asking price just to see what the owners would come back with.

They knocked back the offer and accepted another offer the next day. At first we were a little disappointed but we were sure that we would find the right place for us. We looked at a few other places but none of them felt right. So, we let the idea slide for a couple of weeks, and over that time we both started to question whether we were really disappointed over losing the condo. That place really was exactly what we needed, and when we talked more about it we realised that it checked all our boxes. Another one came up in the same complex but it just wasn't quite the same, and it was a lot more expensive. The one we lost was in the perfect location of the complex, so yes we finally admitted to ourselves that we were totally bummed that we lost it but there was no point dwelling over it, even though we did make comments about it being our home every time we drove past it. Then Kate, being typical Kate with her bold statements, said, 'Well, you never know, settlements fall through all the time, because of financing, they change their mind.' It was a nice thought but we let it go.

A few more weeks went by and we decided it was time to try again. We knew we wanted a place exactly like the one we had lost, and we jumped on the real-estate database – and guess what we found? The original condo – our condo – was still listed. We tried not to get our hopes up as I rang Dennis.

'BARNEY!' he would say through the phone every time I rang. This time he added: 'You won't believe it – your house just came back on the market an hour ago because the finance fell through!'

Kate and I got a bit excited and asked him could we have another look at it that day. We met him at the house a few hours later, had another look through and again we knew it was perfect and already felt like ours. So, we didn't miss it again; we put in an offer and then had to wait for Dennis to call us back once he had an answer. It was the longest two days ever!

Finally the call came from Dennis. 'What do you want to hear?' he said. 'The good news or the bad news?'

Whenever I am asked this question I always want to hear the good news first, so I said, 'Let's start with the good news!'

'All right,' he said. 'Well, the good news is they accepted your offer . . .' Kate and I yelled with excitement. He interrupted by saying, 'But the bad news is you have a ten-day escrow.' This is American real-estate language for settlement. We said without even thinking for a second: 'Done.'

When I ended the call my cheers very quickly turned into an *Oh shit* because even though it was exciting that I'd just bought a condo in America I hadn't told my financial advisor or my bank manager. I actually hadn't even told them I'd been looking for a place. I wish I could have had a camera on the facial reactions when I called them with the news. I knew they weren't so much going to be worried about the fact of buying the place as they were for the short time period I had to gather the funds and have them transferred to California. I'm so lucky to have such a great team behind me, though, and they guided me through those hectic ten days. Papers were emailed between financial advisor and bank, sent to me, printed, signed, scanned, air freighted back to Australia (because it had to be a proper signature not a scanned signature) to my bank, which then had to send them back over to purchase the property. It was touch and go, but we managed to scrape everything together just in time.

So, I had just bought a property in California! That was exciting! Now that we had the house it had to be modified a little to make it accessible. We had the main bedroom downsized a bit to make room for a bigger open ensuite and had to pull out the carpet because it was like pushing my chair through sand. Dennis and Donna knew all sorts of contractors, so pretty soon things were underway.

* * *

Every session we were working hard and trying to get my legs to lock out. We would do it over and over again: stand up, sit down. I had set a goal to be able to lock my legs out by the end of the trip. I kept almost getting it, then my hip flexors would kick in and sniper me back down. I was fighting my body to get it out of its usual seated position, and as the end of our trip approached it still wasn't happening. So, I just kept focusing on the progress that I had made. I think I was actually trying too hard. We realised I was pushing down through Jason's shoulders a lot as I tried to climb my way up to a standing position. The next time I took a deep breath, let go and as we came up, Jason said, 'Barn, you're standing.' He told me to look in the mirror. This was the biggest mind fuck that I had ever had. I could see myself standing but my mind kept questioning it. It was something I had wanted so badly for so long that it felt surreal to actually do it.

The next thing I heard was a sniffle behind me. Kate was in tears just staring at me. It was a really proud moment that soon changed to sadness. Had I really just stood for the first time, the day that I was flying home to Australia? We couldn't extend our trip because of our visas, so it was devastating to have to leave when we had just made such a major breakthrough. But it was also incredible to leave on such a high.

CHAPTER 17

BOHEMIANS

KADA AND BARNEY

When opportunity comes knocking at your door, you best believe you've got to grab it by the horns and jump on for the ride. The unknown is a frightening idea but that's also what makes it so damn cool. When you jump in with zero expectations it opens you up to endless possibilities. It can really lead you anywhere, and that is what life is all about.

BARNEY

The past year – 2010 – had been pretty successful for both of us. I hit a huge milestone of standing, locking out my knees and grounding myself through my feet. It was a feeling I simply cannot describe in words. I always knew I could do it, but to actually get there – I don't think I could have ever truly prepared myself for how good it would feel to reach that goal. And as for Kate: I was so proud that she had finally announced to the world her intention to pursue music as a career – she had even made it Facebook official, which makes it real, right? I know how big a step this was for her but I also knew that she was made for it.

It was a new year, and a big one for us. We were both granted new US visas that allowed us to stay in America for six months a year for five years. We had bought the condo, so we made the big decision to split our time between Sawtell and our new Californian home. Kate's parents agreed to stay in our Sawtell house longer and look after our dogs so we were happy knowing that the house and our babies were in safe hands.

Six months out of Australia each year was going to be a huge adjustment but we knew that it was the right choice. Our experience so far had shown that my body needed the first three months of training to really start to make progress, so I was super pumped to see what I could do over a longer stint.

KADA

We both felt many mixed emotions about the big trip. We knew it was what we needed to do but it was also hard to leave all our friends and family behind, especially Jäger and

Nitro, but it was comforting to know that my family were going to be there for them.

* * *

It was such a surreal feeling to have our own home in California, a place that we had fallen in love with and was now officially our second home. We both felt extremely lucky that of all the places in the world, Project Walk was there, right in the heart of an amazing surf community and small-town feel even though there are 100 000 people. It is also an easy drive into the city chaos of both San Diego and LA but close enough to quickly escape the rat race too. It was great to get a chance to finally meet our neighbours. Most were original owners and it was nice to know that they were there to look out for us and our place.

For the next few years our routine became set: six months at home in Sawtell, which was kind of like our holiday period, then back to Carlsbad where we were locked in for Barney's training on Mondays, Tuesdays, Thursdays and Fridays, leaving us the other days to rest. During our first summer in the US we had tried to squeeze everything into the three-month period but now we had longer to explore, plus we had already done every tourist attraction from San Diego to LA. It was a nice change to have a bit more down time and enjoy our new home. I think it also helped a lot with Barney's therapy. His sessions were ramping up week by week, which was really taxing on his energy. So, his body was definitely in need of rest between sessions. The more progress he made the more in tune he was becoming with his body and its needs. It also pushed us further into wanting to know more and more about how to expand human potential and to question everything.

Things took another greater turn when our friend Jason introduced us to his mum, Marta. Marta is one of the kindest souls we have ever met and very quickly became our American mum. Marta worked in the field of quantum physics and she introduced us to a whole new way of life. Barney had his first session with her and her revolutionary electro-activity patterns biofeedback device, which provides information about your body and reveals anything that is negatively affecting your health, detecting imbalances by responding to the body's electric reactivity patterns. Afterwards my mind was exploding with more understanding than I had ever had. It was like a thousand light bulbs had just been switched on and I was beginning to realise a lot about myself, about Barney and about us as a couple. I had never tried anything like this before. I had been so quick to push Barney into every treatment but I had never felt like I had the right to want to try too. Marta could tell that I was long overdue for some of my own healing, so she welcomed me in with love as I experienced my first session with her. There is a lot of science behind what Marta does yet it also has an undeniable spiritual side. I had been pretty closed off to spirituality up until this point. I didn't understand the difference between it and religion and I had a hard time opening up to anything in that realm because of how it had made me feel when I was growing up. I had a burning desire to simply just be me and have the space to allow me to find who that was. Marta was always very gracious about not putting her own personal beliefs forward on to us but was always ready to discuss anything we were open to. She also lent me a book by Louise Hay called *You Can Heal Your Life*. It was definitely an organic process and the more time I spent with Marta, the essence of her being just filled me with so much positive energy. I wanted to know how I could live like that. Her sessions were kind of like meditative counselling sessions. We would discuss issues that had come up and I started to learn not to dwell on them and simply acknowledge them and let them go. For Barney and me it was the awakening of our true authentic selves and we finally understood the power behind our thoughts and learnt the Law of Attraction, which is: like attracts like, or: what you put out, you attract back in.

We have been blessed by so many incredible people coming into our lives at the exact moment we needed them. Although not everyone is still a part of our life we are truly grateful for them. They are all teachers and reflections of who we were or are in the moment. One of our favourite sayings is, 'When the student is ready the teacher will come.' I can't tell you how true this is. When we shared our goals, out loud in a place of love and safety with the deepest sincerity, the doors began to open. It takes a level of certainty and belief in yourself to choose which door to walk through and it takes bravery to commit to it, but when you allow others to share the journey with you, there is nothing stopping you from reaching your chosen destination.

* * *

BARNEY

After a surf one day, Tim Fox invited me to Taylor Knox's bachelor party, and I was so pumped for it even though the only thing Tim would tell me was that we had a corporate box at the San Diego Padres Major League Baseball game supplied by the Padres. One thing I am so grateful for is that a lot of the guys I looked up to as a grommet, I now call my friends. The party was happening the following weekend and I knew that Mick Fanning was going to be in town, so no doubt it was going to get loose.

We all met at Taylor's house to start and then caught a train down to the game. The crew were a bunch of legends, which spoke volumes about Taylor and the guys he surrounded himself with. During the trip Mick introduced me to Dana, a huge bloke who loved to laugh. We hit it off straightaway and one of the first things I respected about him was that he didn't treat me like I was in a wheelchair. Within a few hours and after a few drinks we became buds. It started out as the occasional slap round the head and turned into a big wrestle on the train with me falling out of my chair and pulling him down with me. Passengers on the train were screaming at him to stop thinking he was beating me up and even had security run from the other end of the train to see what was going on, ready to use force against him. After a late night in which we missed the last connection we had to catch a cab, the brawling continued.

When I got home I kept going on about my new friend. Dana wants to go surfing, Dana this and Dana that. I then crashed out and woke up to a pissed-off Kate. She wouldn't tell me what was up.

'Have I done anything?' I asked.

'No,' she said but she wasn't happy.

I didn't think I'd been that drunk but I hoped I hadn't thrown up or something. She kept telling me it was all good but I could tell she was still upset. The following Friday we were invited to an event where Xavier Rudd was playing. Throughout the night I caught up with a few of the lads from the bachelor party night including Mick reminiscing about the good times. Someone smacked me in the back of the head, so I turned around and it was Dana. I called Kate over and introduced her to him. Throwing him under the bus I said, 'This was the one who led me astray the other night!'

'Fuck off,' he said laughing.

'So, *that's* Dana?' Kate asked later, and it was like a weight had been taken off her.

On the way home she told me she thought the Dana I was raving on about – and so openly telling her about wrestling and mucking around with – was a woman!

From that day on Dana became my main man. He was always keen to take me surfing in California and constantly tried to push me into the biggest and best waves. Well, sometimes I think he'd push me into some just to smash me. That was actually where my motto 'No Means Go' came from. He was a bit hard of hearing in the water because of wearing tack in his ear, and if especially big waves would come and I'd yell, 'No! No! No!' he would take it as, 'Go! Go! Go!' It never ended well. 'No Means Go' then became my motto because in my recovery, whenever anyone would tell me, 'No, you won't be able to do that,' a switch would flick in me to say, 'It's go time!' to prove them wrong.

We started a weekend surf crew, with Dana in charge as my main man. It felt good to have made a solid network of friends in our home away from home. They are as much our best friends as our friends back home. They are all family.

KADA

It was coming up to our four-year anniversary and I was starting to drop some serious hints that I was ready to take the next step in our commitment to each other. Barney had said to me pretty early on, though, that he wouldn't propose to me until he could do it properly on one knee. So, whenever he was training, I would make jokes to his trainers about helping him practise kneeling, but he would quickly shut it down. I had recently watched the royal wedding of Will and Kate and became obsessed with ideas for our magical day. Barney, on the other hand, would barely show even a glimpse of interest. Anyone who knows me, knows that I love to plan a party; it's probably my second favourite passion after music. So, the idea that I could soon be planning the ultimate party of my life had me creating folders all over the desktop of ideas, from rings to dresses to event styling. I know that most girls can relate to this momentary rush of craziness. Patience wasn't and still isn't really my strong point; Barney, in contrast, has the patience game down to a fine art, which is great for him but sometimes exasperating for me. I thought that if I did all the work for him, maybe it would give him a little kickstart. So, I would go in to the jewellery stores to try on rings. I actually found one I became obsessed with: it was a beautiful twisted diamond band with a two-carat solitaire diamond set in the middle. I went into the store alone so many times, I don't think the staff believed that I even had a boyfriend.

Barney thought it was hilarious, and every time I tried to convince him to just look at the ring he would change the subject or tell me we weren't ready yet. I knew his reasons, but it infuriated me. A girl just can't help herself when that engagement alarm goes off in her mind. He kept telling me that he would ask me when I stopped bugging him about it. Honestly, I didn't think that was an option, though – when I get passionate about an idea, that's it.

I held out for a year dropping hints, but then I was ready to put it to rest and so decided to give it one last go. We had met a couple who had just celebrated their tenth wedding anniversary, for which the husband bought his wife a yellow diamond ring. Yellow diamond? I had never seen anything so beautiful. Right then, I knew that was the style of ring I had been searching for, though maybe a few carats smaller than her six. I knew everything there was to know about a regular clear diamond and I had even made an information sheet for Barney. I was also very conscious about finding an ethically sourced diamond. I began my research on yellow canary diamonds and found a reputable dealer from Israel. I began corresponding with one of the employees and she helped me not only pick the perfect diamond but also design a ring. I gave her my ring size and she sent me a quote with everything included. I forwarded the email on to Barney, which I saw he immediately trashed. Again that made me mad because of the amount of work I put into it. I felt about this ring the same way I did about the condo. Big call, I know, but that was how I genuinely felt. I kept checking the site, only to find that the diamond had been reserved. I remember freaking out and telling Barney that we should just tell her that we would take it and he could just keep it for when he was ready. Of course, Barney laughed at me and said once again, 'No, Kate, we're not ready yet.'

This caused a big argument. I was hurt and confused about why he would say we weren't ready. I knew he meant that he wasn't ready yet because he had set a goal, but it still hurt a lot. So, I forced myself to let it go.

* * *

I'd bought tickets to an LA Lakers game as a birthday present for Barney earlier in the year. The crowd was electric and we had the best time. During the heartwarming deliverance of the US anthem, 'The Star Spangled Banner', I couldn't help but gush about how powerful it was. I said to Barney, 'I know I'm Australian but one day I would love to sing that for a major event.' You know those bold statements that I keep telling you about? Well, yep it happened again. Two weeks later we arrived at training and Gigi, who was in charge of client relations and fundraising, asked me to come into her office. They were holding a fundraising event at Petco Stadium, home of the San Diego Padres Major League Baseball Team, during spinal awareness month in September. As part of their involvement, she had to nominate someone to sing the national anthem. 'Would you be interested?' she asked. WHAT?! 'Can I even do that?' I replied in a rush. 'I'm not

American.' She said she had already run it by the organisers and they were okay with it as long as I passed the audition.

I ran to tell Barney the news, but of course he already knew. He reminded me of what I had said only a couple of weeks before at the Lakers game. We couldn't believe that it was actually going to happen. This is how we saw in full effect the importance of sharing goals with others. There is something magic that happens when you say it out loud and speak of it passionately. I realised that everything I had ever manifested came from a place of imagination. It was my mini me speaking through. My goals always seemed pretty far-fetched but the trick was that I never became attached to the outcomes. I'd say it in a daze of romance as I imagined what the idea would be like in reality and then as quickly as I thought of it, I'd let it go.

It really got me wondering, though. If I had been able to manifest all these amazing things into my life kind of by accident, then how could I do it on purpose? This has been a daily struggle ever since. It takes true patience, trust and faith as well as an ability to imagine the goal as if it has already been reached. That part I have down, but the patience and trust is where I need a little more work.

I had three months to plan for the anthem, but first I had to make it through the audition. We drove down to San Diego and I met with the Padres' event coordinator. Thankfully I breezed through the audition, and it was time to memorise the words and then the pronunciation and then the timing. I was given a window of one minute fifteen seconds to complete the song. Even Americans have been known to get it wrong. Some of the greatest performers of all time have made mistakes and been ridiculed by the public. Being an Australian, I was terrified of getting it wrong. The last thing I wanted to do was offend anyone. So, I practised and practised for three months straight. Our neighbours must have thought I was incredibly patriotic.

BARNEY

I knew pretty early on that one day I was going to marry Kate. When we started getting serious, I told her that I wouldn't propose until I could kneel down to do it. It was a goal I had set for myself and one I hoped she would support. Of course she said that it didn't matter to her but she knew how much it meant to me.

My training was going really well and our relationship was getting better and stronger. We were coming up to five years and Kate was more than ready to get engaged. It was so funny how annoyed she would get when I ignored her emails and texts – all containing photos of diamond rings. Okay, it's not really that funny, but kind of. The thing is, I love giving surprises and I'm actually really good at it. Kate is impatient, so she loves them as long as she has no idea that there is one coming her way.

I had been practising my standing and it was starting to get really solid. During one of my sessions with Mica, she felt that my body was totally switched on, so she asked if Kate would like to swap out and stand with me. It's really hard for Kate to hide her excitement – she wears her heart on her sleeve; it's one of the things I love about her – and as she and Mica swapped places I looked down at the biggest smile I had ever seen. We had been talking about this moment for nearly five years, and it was all that we had hoped it would be. To be able to hold her as I looked down into her eyes – it was perfect. Every day and every milestone with her was getting better and better. I knew in that moment that I was going to ask her to marry me.

She had emailed me an order form with the diamond and ring setting she wanted. She had already done everything, it was just a matter of me going ahead with it. As soon as she sent it through I put it in another folder in my inbox that I knew she would never look in: Bills. I corresponded with the diamond dealer in Israel and bought the diamond, and I told her that if Kate emailed her, she was to tell her that the diamond had been sold. She was very helpful and excited to get things going.

When we found out that Kate had been nominated to sing the national anthem at the Padres game I knew I had found the date I would ask her. I told Gigi my plans and she was happy to help out in any way she could to make it perfect for us. I needed an address to send the ring to, so I had it addressed to Gigi at Project Walk and she organised to hold it in the safe for me until the big day.

Everything was on track until Kate, being Kate, tried on Mica's ring while I was training one day. Mica has small fingers, but her ring fitted Kate. Kate said, 'That's weird, I thought I was a bigger size than that.'

I freaked out straightaway and immediately emailed the jeweller to change the size of Kate's ring. Luckily it was all fine.

Like I said before, I am pretty good at surprises, so I kept pretty tight-lipped about my plan. The only person who knew was Gigi because I needed to request a money withdrawal to purchase the ring without Kate knowing. As the time came closer I told one of my trainers, Eric, that I wanted to kneel for the proposal so we needed to practise. The issue with this was that Kate was at all my training sessions, so I never got a chance to practise.

In the weeks leading up to the day Gigi and I were secretly making plans about the details of the proposal. I had tried to get clearance to do it on the field straight after she sang and have it on the big screen, but apparently too many girls had said no to proposals, so the organisers no longer allowed it. So, I went to plan B: I would ask her on the rooftop of the Western Metal building that overlooked the stadium, where the fundraiser event would be held, right after she sang.

The big day arrived and I had to play it cool to not let on that I was totally freaking out. She was nervous but excited to get onto the field. We had invited all our friends down to the game;

they were coming to support the fundraising event but also to see Kate sing the anthem. It was a pretty big deal, and everyone was gearing up for a good night. As we arrived, I stopped Kate and gave her a kiss. 'Tonight will be amazing,' I told her. The best part was her not knowing how amazing it actually would be.

She was called to the field, mic in hand, and there she sang what has been described as the best US anthem that many had ever heard. I knew she had it in her but it was an awesome feeling to watch her nail it in front of twenty-five-plus thousand people.

As we made our way up to the rooftop to watch the game, everyone was raving about her voice and her delivery of the song. She was on a high and I was about to make it even better.

I had organised a distraction for Kate while the girls set up for me. This was it. Game time. They rolled out a red carpet and scattered it with rose petals. Eric and another trainer Sachi lifted me out of my chair and put me into a kneeling position. We couldn't believe how seamless it was. We hadn't had a chance to practise, so we had to just go for it, and it worked. I had the ring box and by that point everyone but Kate knew what was about to happen. Everything was ready for her, so Gigi told Kate that I was looking for her and she needed to come.

Someone hit play on the iPod and through the speakers came the song that Kate had played to me over and over again, singing to me every word: 'Marry Me' by Train. As she walked around the corner we made eye contact, and that first look of sincere surprise was what I had planned for. She walked down the carpet crying, which made me cry too. Everyone was cheering and clapping for us. She finally got to me and I handed her the ring and said, 'Say you will,' she lent down gave me a kiss and said 'YES!' That night was all time.

KADA

First of all I want to know how the hell Barney managed to slip this surprise straight past me, but I am so happy he did because it was the ultimate surprise. I was nervous all day for the anthem and I think even a bit stressfully snappy towards Barney, but he was very supportive the whole way.

Singing the anthem in front of a crowd of more than 25 000 people was seriously a highlight of my life. The energy on that field was so powerful, and once I started to sing all the nerves and fears just fell away. It was a moment for which I will be forever grateful.

When we got to the top floor of the Western Metal building, I was starving. I don't think I had eaten all day because my nerves were running too high. I had just sat down to eat when Gigi came to grab me and told me there were a few people who wanted to speak to me. So, I left my plate and followed her. As I spoke to a few people about my music and the process of the anthem, I started to wonder why Gigi had pulled me away. I also noticed a cameraman following me but just assumed it was because I sang the anthem and they were getting footage of the fundraiser. I never imagined it was for what was about to happen.

Gigi then came back and told me that Barney was looking for me and that he needed me. I excused myself from the conversation and went to find him. As I turned the corner, all eyes were on me. I looked down to see him kneeling at the end of a red carpet covered with rose petals, and I heard the song playing that I had sung to him on repeat as I bugged him to marry me. Finally it was him asking me.

I was so proud of him. I knew how much that goal to kneel meant to him, and he did it. That yes was the greatest and most sure yes of my life. It suddenly occurred to me that everyone had been filming. I quickly yelled out for no-one to post anything online until I called my mum. Of course our families were thrilled but not really surprised. How could I have been the only one totally unaware? It really was the perfect night.

We were both the happiest we had ever been, and after talking it over we decided to hold off the wedding until Barney could complete his next goal: to stand at the altar while my dad walked me down the aisle, and to share our first dance. I was so excited to officially be able to start planning a wedding. We decided on early 2015. That gave us three years to plan and for Barney to train for his big goal.

CHAPTER 18

NO MEANS GO

We tried and we tried but we can't let go.
They say it can't be done but we need to know for sure.
There's always got to be that one to break down that
door, why can't it be we?
We're shooting down impossible.

– Kada, 'Shooting Down Impossible'

BARNEY

At the end of 2012, I was approached by some film students from New York to do a story on my recovery. They had heard how well I was doing and wanted me to be the subject of their final project. After the school told them they couldn't come to Australia to film their project, they opted to come anyway on their own dime and make my story their first project out of school. They became Trinity Film Productions.

They came out for the Quiksilver Pro at Snapper Rocks on the Gold Coast and then to cover my charity contest, the Barney Miller Classic. As they started to capture their interviews from friends from the surf tour and then friends from home, the story really started to take shape and grow. They had heard that Kate and I had just got engaged and my new goal was to stand at the altar and have our first dance, so they asked if we would be interested in them following the progress of that journey. We were stoked to have them be part of it but very quickly warned them that the time frame was going to be years rather than weeks or months. They still wanted to go ahead, so we started the 'No Means Go' campaign, a documentary on my life and recovery to show people what is possible, and that you can still live a pretty rad life despite the cards you have been dealt. Committing to this film was one of the best things I could have done. It kept me accountable for my goals and it became more than just about me. It was the chance to show the world what the human body is really capable of.

KADA

After a few months of searching the internet for the perfect wedding location I came across a home north of Coffs Harbour in Woolgoolga. Marlowe House is on a twelve-acre property located on the beach and is a beautiful timber-weatherboard bohemian-style home. We made an appointment to meet the property manager out there one beautiful afternoon, and driving in took my breath away. It was so lush with green lawns and had a country-on-the-beach vibe. We fell in love with the place instantly. The home itself is huge but what we loved was the large wide open space for our guests. We had our hearts set on an outdoor wedding that would reflect us as the couple we are, and the property represented that perfectly. At the time the house hadn't been used often for weddings but it was beginning to gain more popularity and I asked if booking two years in advance would be classed as bridezilla behaviour; the property manager laughed and said, 'No way.' So, we booked: 18 April 2015. Even though there were still a few years to go, I knew it was going to take a lot of planning and I wanted to plan every detail. I hired a wedding planner, Lauren, from North Coast Luxury Weddings and an event stylist, Kiri, from Rosie Pose Event Hire to help us dream up the perfect event.

BARNEY

We saw a lot of changes in 2014. I had started working with Josh a lot more on the previous trip because Jason was out recovering from shoulder surgery and Mica was pregnant. We formed a really strong friendship and my body was responding well to everything he was trying. We bonded over surfing and I even surprised him one day by bringing Mick Fanning in for a training session. That was a special day.

Most of my trainers from Project Walk were moving on to new things. Mica had a baby girl and Josh and the training-floor manager Jason left and opened up a new centre in San Juan Capistrano called Strides. It was time for a change and to ruffle up my program a bit. There is no room for growth in the comfort zone.

I decided not to go back to Project Walk when I returned to California and I followed Josh and Jason to their new venture at Strides. What they have created there is amazing, and we are proud to be part of the Strides family. Josh has so much knowledge of the body and an awesome gift for what he does. He takes the lead from my body to determine where the session will go, instead of simply running through a regular program. Back at Project Walk Josh had taught Kate how to stand transfer me, which totally changed our lives. That alone kept my body in good shape while I was home and instead of the usual few weeks to adjust, this time round my body was on from day one.

KADA

We had heard of another place back in Australia called NeuroPhysics Therapy and its founder Ken Ware. Ken with his ground-breaking therapy was having great success with not only spinal injuries but numerous other chronic disorders as well. We had been put on the waiting list to see Ken and finally got the call that an opening was available. We were excited to try something new and see where it led us but sad that it meant we had to cut short our trip to Strides and our work with Josh.

We had no idea what to expect but we had been looking for the next phase in Barney's recovery program. We knew we needed something more than just physical training, he needed his mind to let go of the stresses and trauma that were potentially holding him back.

We arrived with no expectations; I think that's what made it exciting. A unique part of the therapy, from what we had seen, was when the patient's nervous system seemed to be taken into a form of neural tremor. This, it seems, opens up the pathways and begins to create new ones. We had no idea how the tremor would start, nor how intense it would be, or if it would hurt, but we were keen to find out.

Ken welcomed us to the facility and showed us the equipment. He explained that the tremor is self-triggered under a state of super-relaxation, whilst introducing and self-administering a mild stress into the nervous system. The best way to explain it simply is to think of the uncontrollable shake you get when you hold a hard exercise like a squat or lunge or even a sit-up. That shake is the tremor, but the big difference is that this form of tremor emerges under quite the opposite conditions: you are super-relaxed and moving light weights very slowly on special exercise machines, which creates and maintains the necessary parameters for the nervous system to recalibrate to. Ken describes this as 'working through the grids', which allows for accurate assessments of positive changes a person's nervous system has undergone. Through years of study Ken has discovered that if you induce this form of tremor and provide some online cognitive guidance, it opens up your body to repair and evolve as a result of the individual's progressive cognitive removal of inhibitions and restraints. The paradox is that you gain control by not trying to control it. However, you *are* in control because you are telling yourself to let it go – just be present and let the nervous system do its thing.

BARNEY

Ken started by talking me into a calm meditative head space, which is where you gain full composure over your thoughts and the situation. Your mind knows that you are not in danger but your body doesn't, so it responds accordingly. I didn't know how hard it would be to go into the tremor. Ken told me not to worry about it because it usually takes patients a day or two to be able to let go. Not me, though – within minutes I was shaking all over the place. My body must have been ready for the upgrade.

The next day Ken's wife, Nickie, took Kate through the program so she could feel what I was feeling and also understand it for herself a bit better. Over the course of four days my body started to feel different. I felt more connected to it than I ever had. I booked in to return again a month later for another four-day intensive block.

On my second visit to Ken he connected me to a machine with electrode pads which collected data on how my body responded to the various phases of tremor. I had pads stuck to my inner thighs, outer thighs, abs and shoulders. For the first time ever I was able to see in full scientific proof that my body had clear signals throughout its entirety. We just needed to flood that signal more to make the messages more fluid. Since my accident I had steered clear of science and the medical world when it came to my recovery because they had always said that there was no way of recovering, and I couldn't let that thought enter my mind. Through working with Ken I learnt how important the belief system is. It has the ability to create disease as much as it does to reverse it. This was exactly the next step I'd needed, and I was ready to move forward.

CHAPTER 19

WHAT DOESN'T KILL YOU MAKES YOU STRONGER

Will you take my heart, while I take your pain?
Will you hear my stories of where I've been?
Yes your world was yours but now let it be mine,
You're not alone cause anywhere you go I'll follow.

– Kada 'I'll Follow'

KADA AND BARNEY

There are moments in your life that downright suck and you are
often left wondering what is the point of it all? What is the grand
plan behind it? Why do we have to fall in order to rise? The answer
is simple, it's life. All reminders that we are human and to not
take this life for granted. Use every experience good and bad as an

opportunity for growth because when you cannot see that, you are
missing the point of it all.

BARNEY

It has never been a case of smooth sailing for me, but I also now understand that every turbulent moment we live through is another opportunity to change the way you have been doing things and do them better. I had a lot of stress on my plate. We were into the final six months before the wedding. We sold our family home while our new dream home was being built across the road. We had been busy filming the documentary and then to top it all off the woman I drew all my strength from, who taught me life – my mum – was starting to slip away from us; she was diagnosed with early-stage dementia.

I ended up in the emergency room at Coffs Harbour Hospital late one night in the most excruciating pain I had ever known. It felt like someone had a dagger in my side and was sliding it in and out. I was suffering from Autonomic Dysreflexia, something I hadn't experienced since the early days of my injury. I was having trouble regulating my blood pressure, it was going through waves of skyrocketing and setting off the alarms at 240/170 to then dropping excessively low, which made it hard for the doctors to medicate. They established that I had a chronic infection in my right kidney that they had to address in the hope of stabilising everything else. They ended up having to intravenously inject me with an antibiotic for it to have a faster release. Thankfully after a few days the infection broke and I was cleared to move out of intensive care and into the medical ward.

Over the weekend I had scans and ultrasounds to find the source of the problem. The results came back with a bladder stone the size of a golf ball. A few days later, when I was no longer at risk of an emergency, I was transferred to Baringa Private Hospital and prepped for surgery. I was made aware by the surgeon that there was a high chance that I was going to have to have two surgeries because of the size of the stone.

Just as they suspected after the first surgery, I needed another one but had a few days to recover in between. The good news was that Kate could stay with me. After the previous hectic few months it was kind of like a holiday for us both, even if it was in a hospital and I had nearly died. It was nice, the staff were super friendly and the food was surprisingly good. I actually looked forward to getting my menu every day. We watched tonnes of movies but mostly it was nice to be forced to do nothing. It also gave us time to finish off our wedding invitations: they were chocolate bars including a Wonka's Golden Ticket, to go with our theme of Pure Imagination.

The second surgery was a success, they were able to break down and remove the remainder of the stone and it was now time to rest and recover fully.

KADA

It's heartbreaking to watch someone you love suffer through so much pain. Barney never complains about pain, he sees it as a blessing that he can feel something and he pushes through it, but this time was different. He was scared and he cried over and over to make it stop. It crushed me. A man I thought was almost invincible was close to leaving me forever. I had dealt with a lot of loss, but this one would have broken me and I don't think I would have ever recovered. I had tried to be strong for him but he could see through it; he knows me too well.

I pushed to stay with him the entire time. Every time he would have a Dysreflexic episode I had to sit him up to help alleviate the pressure. Reaction to the symptoms is very time critical, so I told the hospital staff that I would be there to take that extra stress off them and also to alert them if needed because once an episode started he was out of it and couldn't press the alarm button. I slept in a chair beside his bed but was woken every five minutes by alarms and beeps of the machines. Because of Barney's condition they couldn't get a stable blood pressure reading, so it would alert the nurses frequently to come check on him. Once they found an appropriate antibiotic to give to him intravenously his fever thankfully broke and he started to fight off the infection in his kidney.

I worried for him, I worried that he wasn't going to make it through the first surgery let alone the second. I always find the positive in everything but I suddenly couldn't see it. I didn't want to even imagine what my life would be like without him in it. I didn't tell our friends and families how close he came to leaving us because I didn't want to say it out loud. I didn't want to break, because I was trying so hard to keep it together for him.

Helen, Barney's mum, had been showing signs of dementia over the previous year. Day by day she was slipping away from us. This was the breaking point for Barney. I think the reason he had never gone through depression from his accident was because he knew he had power of his mind and his choices, but to not have control over the health of someone he truly loves devastated him.

BARNEY

Losing my mum this slow cruel way to this heartless disease has been extremely hard to come to terms with. Although she is still here with us, it kills me to see her in this way. The hardest part of our whole journey has been accepting that although we have had an awakening of a new way of life and found new understanding and a world of amazing knowledge, we can only lead by example and hope that others follow in our footsteps. We had a really hard time accepting that there was nothing we could do for Mum. We searched high and low for answers to all of our questions and found a lot of positive information about lifestyle and diet; we wanted to change her whole life because we were so desperate to save her. The thing that took us a long time to understand was that at the end of the day it wasn't just our decision. We're still on an emotional roller-coaster; there are days we visit her and we leave crying and asking ourselves if this is really how it has to be. We've watched the most intelligent woman I know, the woman who raised me and taught me to fight, slowly forget how to do everything she loved. Write, read and even hold a conversation. I guess I hit breaking point. I was emotionally drained, and tired of trying so hard to then be knocked down again. I had always had my mum to tell me everything was going to be okay, but this time was different. I suddenly had to be that strength for her and I didn't know how when I was falling apart too. I hated that I couldn't help her and the thought of her missing out on all my achievements that she supported me through shattered me.

We took my mum to the wedding location so she could be familiar with it before the wedding day. We were determined for mum to be part of our day. She had been so excited for us before she got sick and we knew she would want to be there. The one thing we are truly grateful for is that she is happy and still knows the people she loves and who love her. This is all we want, for her to be surrounded by love. I am also eternally grateful to her husband, my step-dad, Mal. He has shown his unconditional love for her and stood by her every step of the way. We are so blessed to have him in our lives.

KADA

It was tough to watch Barney lose his zest for life. He didn't want to do anything. He didn't want to stand, or train. He just wanted to mourn the mother he once knew, but it was hard for him because he wasn't ready to let go. We weren't ready to let go. All we could do was simply love her. Even though at the time it felt like we needed to do more, to her that love was everything.

We were so grateful that our beautiful friends Dean and Tracey bought our home. It was one of those perfect moments where you get to choose your neighbours because we were going to be moving across the street once our new home was built. They were kind enough to let us stay in the house with them while we waited for our home to be ready, which ended up being seven months. It was seven months that saved us.

Dean and Trace have three incredibly beautiful kids. Lilly, who was seven, Grace, five and James, one – they had this fearless energy that totally brightened up our days. Their view of the world was innocent and imaginative and the fact that they thought we were cool – well, that made us feel pretty cool too. Having them as a constant in our lives helped us heal, especially Barney. Watching the way they took on life gave him the courage to get back up too and fight for the life that he had been dreaming of.

I think the icing on the cake was a little reminder from our friend Mick. In 2013 he won his third Surfing World Title and during his acceptance speech at the ASP (Association of Surfing Professionals, which is now World Surf League) banquet he told a story of the day he went to watch Barney train. He spoke about watching him walk assisted in his walker and how it brought tears to his eyes and inspired him to know that no-one can tell you no. He then thanked Barney and said it was the highlight of his year.

Watching this stirred something in Barney. Mick was not only a great friend to us but someone we looked up to, someone who also knows how to turn tragedy into triumph.

BARNEY

For the first time ever, I didn't see a way out. At least not on my own. I didn't know if I even had it in me to stand and dance at our wedding. The thought of letting everyone down terrified me. This day meant so much more than just me standing; it was a day to celebrate our life together and the journey it had taken to get there. What if I couldn't do it?

I stayed in bed for months, barely leaving. Having the kids around definitely saved me. Their infectious laughter and drive for life made it hard to stay sad. They were so fierce and unapologetic of being exactly who they wanted to be. It was refreshing and reminded us both to not take things so seriously and just have fun.

After a few pep talks with Ken and easing back into training, the dark fog began to lift. I got back in contact with a friend Clint, from my teenage years. We used to hang out and surf together and then he moved away to pursue a career in rugby league. After a successful career in both the top leagues in Australia and in Europe he had retired and was moving home. He had been studying for a degree in human movement and came from a family of extremely switched-on people, all working in the field of holistic wellbeing. I told him my goals and that I was looking for a trainer with an open mind who could learn my programs and also add their own knowledge. He came and learnt from Ken and we also FaceTimed with Josh to get tips from him. It felt good to finally have someone to train me at home after all these years. That drive that I had tucked away for a few months welcomed me back like a long-lost friend and I was ready to get back to work. It was game on!

KADA

I seem to thrive in a chaotic lifestyle. I love a good project, and for some reason I thought doing them all at once was a great idea. We had been busy with plans for our wedding, which was getting bigger and bigger by the day, and our dream home was finally ready to move into. They say you can really test a relationship by either building a house or planning a wedding and we chose to do both at once. I was also about to launch my debut album, which I had been working on for two years, and we were dealing with Barney's health scare and Helen's health decline, then Barney regaining strength for his training, all while shooting our film. It was a hectic time but more proof of how solid Barney and I are in ourselves and in our relationship.

The good news was that we were ready to move into our dream home. Barney's step-dad, Mal, being a draughtsman, helped us design the house and we were very particular in every detail. We put in a concrete magnesium lap pool next to Barney's gym. We love hosting dinners and parties, so the whole house was designed around entertaining. We felt extremely blessed to be starting our marriage and the next phase of our lives together in a home that was not only completely accessible for Barney's stage of recovery but also a home in which we would one day raise our kids. We had so many great memories from our old home but it was time to move on and we loved that we could still make new memories in it with our friends who bought it.

The wedding was fast approaching and it was time for us to celebrate with our friends. I had chosen five bridesmaids, Candace my maid of honour, Emma, Kelly, Hannah and Bec. The girls planned an incredible hens' getaway for me in the hills of Byron Bay at the most beautiful house I had ever seen. It was a Moroccan-style home with lush gardens and a divine pool area. We sipped on sorbet champagne cocktails all afternoon by the pool and then ended the night with a delicious five-course dinner. It was perfect.

BARNEY

My bucks' day was a little more R-rated than the girls' fancy affair. My seven groomsmen, Toby the best man, Milka, Chaddy, Hiddo, Marto, Grohl and Joe along with another thirty mates took me camping at our favourite spot an hour's drive south of Sawtell. We started the trip with some good waves and then it was party time. There is a certain guy code that you have to abide by when it comes to a bucks' party, so I won't give away any of the details, but let's just say it was wild and I got set on fire during a particular show. I'll leave it to you to use your imagination for the rest.

CHAPTER 20

PURE IMAGINATION

KADA

The wedding weekend had finally arrived. Our friends and families were all beginning to arrive in town and I could not believe that everything on my checklist had been ticked off. We had booked Marlowe House for the weekend and we invited the bridal party to stay with us there for the Friday and Saturday night. We all met out at the house on Friday afternoon to run through the logistics and a rehearsal of the day. The marquees were already up and all the major furniture was in place. After we finalised the last details we had a big dinner with everyone and made a toast for the weekend. The boys planned for a dawn patrol surf session and we girls were looking forward to a morning walk and yoga session before starting on our hair and make-up.

Barney and I aren't very traditional, we slept in the same bed that night and said our last goodnight before becoming husband and wife. I tossed and turned all night. I was exhausted but so excited for the following day that I could hardly sleep. I felt like a kid on Christmas Eve waking every hour to see if it was too early to get up to open presents. I kept waking Barney to tell him how excited I was, but he pretty much ignored me.

It was still dark when I woke and checked the time: it was coming on to 5am. That was good enough for me. I sprang up and got dressed, then kissed Barney and left for our morning walk on the beach. The sunrise did not disappoint.

Even though so much detail and planning went into this day I was a pretty relaxed bride. I didn't have any bridezilla moments but I think it was because of how much time I put into the planning. It wasn't rushed and I knew what we wanted. Barney was also pretty involved, which made it special. It was actually his idea to theme the wedding 'Pure Imagination', from the original Gene Wilder movie – our favourite – *Willy Wonka and the Chocolate Factory*. When I asked Barney what he wanted for the wedding he replied, 'I want a Willy Wonka dessert buffet.'

I replied, 'Okay, so a dessert bar. What kind of desserts?'

His reply was: 'No, I want to re-create the chocolate factory and walk into a room and have everything edible, just like in the movie.'

If you had seen his face, you would have known he had never been so serious. A lot of people say a wedding is for the bride, that it should be the day of her childhood dreams, but in fact our wedding represented us in the perfect way. We don't live a traditional life, so we didn't want a traditional wedding. We were lucky to have friends who helped create the desserts and candy and bring Barney's vision to life.

My hairdresser and friend Narelle is also an amazing yoga teacher and she arrived early to take us girls through a class to unwind and energise for the big day ahead. After yoga we had a big breakfast then the prepping began. The girls popped the champagne and the day officially kicked off.

The boys were stoked that when they got back from the surf, the surf event at Margaret River was on. So, their morning was set in front of the giant projector screen in the main living room of the house. We had timed the wedding around the event so that some of the boys from the tour could make it, but unfortunately the schedule changed after we sent the invitations out. It was amazing that the contest was on that day, and for Barney and the boys to be able to watch it all day still felt like a nice way to have the guys that couldn't make it be part of our special day.

It was incredible to walk around watching everyone put together a vision that I had created in my mind. Our wedding planner had recruited extra staff for the event, and the stylist was busy making everything look beautiful. Our amazing floral queen, Nic, and her husband, Mick, had created the most perfect climbing flower masterpiece on the tree that we were to be married under. We didn't want a formal sit-down meal, so we opted for food stations spread around the reception area for the guests to help themselves. We had Italian, Moroccan, Japanese, and fish and chips, along with our signature cocktails for the night: Moscow Mules in copper mugs.

BARNEY

We woke up to an epic day ahead. Kate was up super early, which meant she must have been excited because she is not a morning person, at all. A big group of us boys headed to the surf for a sunrise session. The waves were fun, it was super glassy and perfect conditions. We had the whole place to ourselves for the best start to the day.

We arrived back at the house to find that the event at Margaret River was on. We got it playing on the big screen as the girls were making breakfast. This day just kept getting better and better. After breakfast, Ken and Clint came to the house to do some training with me. Toby came and helped me practise standing for the ceremony. It was a surreal moment, drinking beers watching the surfing with so many good mates to soak up the good times, including Taylor Steele, one of the most iconic surf filmmakers, and Benji Weatherley, who is in a lot of his movies. We all used to have those movies on repeat, and now these blokes were our mates and I was honoured to have them there to celebrate the day with us.

Soon it was time for us to get ready, and that's when we hit a snag. As we dressed in our suits I realised I had never tried on my pants. They were too small. Our photographer laughed; with all the detail that had gone into this day he couldn't believe that the groom's pants didn't fit. Usually I just wouldn't do them up – no-one would notice if I just stayed in my chair, but seeing as I had to stand for the ceremony and dance I had to just suck it in and hold my breath.

To go with the theme of the day I wore a magenta purple velvet Tom Ford jacket with a white shirt and black pants and a lollipop in place of a lapel pin, a black bow tie, yellow-and-pink shoes gifted from our friends at Senso, and a black top hat. The boys were in white shirts with black pants, black suspenders and magenta purple bow ties. This was it, we were all ready and after a few group photos it was time for us to make our way down to the ceremony. Before I got to the end of the aisle, there in the front row sat my mum and Mal. She came over to give me a hug. It really was the perfect day, she told me she loved me and looked so happy. There is no doubt in my mind that she knew what we were there for and it meant the world to Kate and me to have her there to share this special day.

KADA

Everyone's hair and make-up was done, all that was left to do was get dressed. My champagne silk gown and lace veil were custom made by my friend Jade Kohl, and I had velvet magenta heels to match Barney's jacket. Barney had given me a diamond ring that belonged to his mum, and we had it melted and redesigned by a local jeweller Matt Loretan. We designed a gold hammered band with a solitaire diamond set into the band.

It was an amazing moment when I first saw myself in the mirror. This day had once seemed so far away, and to be standing there ready to walk down the aisle to the love of my life – well, that was a dream come true.

My dad came to give me a kiss and then he took my hand as we made our way to the ceremony. It was such a beautiful experience to share with my dad, those final steps before we walked down the aisle. He told me he loved me and was proud of me, and then the music began.

My heart was filled with so much love and joy when I saw Barney standing there, assisted by Toby and Chaddy; waiting for me. I know how hard it is for him to stand, and I knew he did it for us, and I was so proud. As I walked down the aisle to Ben Harper's 'Forever', sung by our friend Ned, I looked around at everyone I loved with a smile of complete gratitude. I made it to the end, where my dad gave Barney a hug, their first standing hug, and then he gave me a hug and a kiss.

We had asked our amazing friend Quinny to marry us. (We also had an official celebrant there too, to legally officiate the marriage.) We were so honoured to have him be part of our day. We chose to write our own vows, which put the perfect final touch on the ceremony.

BARNEY'S VOWS

Kate, I never thought in a million years that I would be marrying that cute girl that I met at the Sawtell Chilli Festival back in 2007. I have to pinch myself every day when I wake up and see you lying next to me. I want to always look beside me and have you there next to me wherever this life decides to take us. I want us to be that couple that really does stay together, where everyone is like, 'Wow, they're still together?' I never want to stop falling in love with you.

I promise to love and protect you while you're with me and I promise to support you to succeed in whatever you do. I also promise to always be here in times of need. We have seen the best and worst of each other and I choose both. It doesn't matter what our future holds as long as I have you. I love you.

KADA'S VOWS

Barney, I have imagined this moment over and over in my head ever since the first time that we said I love you. You have been my best friend, my lover, my number one supporter, my comfort, my stability and you are now my everything. Every moment with you is a precious gift that I am so grateful for and I am the lucky one to call you mine. I am who I am because of you and get to do what I love because of you. Because you have always believed in me even when I didn't. You have taught me to never be afraid to try. I promise to be the best wife I can possibly be and always be someone that you are proud of. I can't promise that I will always be the best housewife, but in our new home with my trusty new Dyson I am definitely going to have fun trying. I promise to love you forever and forever chase our dreams together, it will always be you and me.

KADA AND BARNEY

After the exchange of the rings, Quinny pronounced us husband and wife and we shared our magical kiss.

The celebrations began and the drinks flowed. As the sun set the guests made their way from cocktail hour to the reception. Leigh Webber, our wonderful MC, introduced the bridal party. They each came down the stairs standing in a line side by side facing everyone.

The lights shut off and this was our cue to get in place. With the words, 'Hold your breath,' one lot of lights came back on. Then, with the next line, 'Make a wish,' the next lights turned on. And with, 'Count to three,' each of the bridal party separated in a twirl to reveal the magic moment: our first dance.

We danced to the song 'Pure Imagination' by Gene Wilder, also from Willy Wonka. *We held each other tight, swaying side to side, gazing into each other's eyes. The song sums up perfectly everything that is our life.*

KADA

There was definitely magic in the air that night. In those five minutes, nothing else existed but us. We had dreamt of this moment, this feeling; we had imagined this night and the reality of it was so much more than we could have ever hoped for. This was actually our first ever dance, the first time Barney had stood for so long without the safety of a chair behind him to catch him, and the first time sharing a dance with our friends and families. That night was definitely a night worth waiting for.

Traditionally, the wedding couple cut the cake to celebrate their union. Instead we cut the ribbon to open Wonka's Dessert Tent. Oh my God! It was a sweet tooth's heaven. In the centre was a five-tier chocolate fountain and dipping station. White chocolate mousse formed the spots of the giant mushrooms amid chocolate brownie dirt with snakes, sour worms and red frogs. A doughnut surfboard that spelt 'B + K' sat amid giant gummy bears, cotton candy trees, croquembouche, tree stumps with an array of caramel tarts, sour strap trees and lollipop trees. It was seriously insane, and we were all living our childhood dreams.

To end the best day of our life, Kid Mac performed while we newlyweds crowd-surfed above the mosh pit. He closed the night with a bang! And that night we went to sleep as Mr and Mrs Miller.

CHAPTER 21

YOU AND ME ... AND BEYOND

BARNEY

We had been filming our documentary, *No Means Go*, for the past few years, but after meeting with the head and co-founder of Garage Entertainment, Mick Lawrence, we changed the direction of the film. Mick's vision of the story was of our love and life together. *No Means Go* was a bit too aggressive for the title of a love story, so we took the final three words from Kate's wedding vows: *You and Me*.

KADA

It was one thing to showcase Barney's journey to recovery but it was a big decision to put not only our lives but also our relationship up for public scrutiny. But after some time thinking it over we knew it was all or nothing. We chose to do it for our families and for all the young boys and girls out there who are struggling through life and think that they can't find a way out. We wanted to share with people what we have learnt: that love comes in many forms, and that it really is as simple as love is love. We wanted to share its power and its ability to heal when you're open to let it in. And we wanted to shed light on the importance of connecting with others, sharing your goals, your pain and all that you are. We have never been so connected like we are today via social media yet we have also never been so disconnected from ourselves and each other.

After four years of filming, we premiered *You and Me* to the world. That experience has given us both so much. It has opened doors to incredible opportunities and it has helped us connect with people in a brand-new way. We now take the film through high schools; the students watch the film, and we go in for a chat and a Q and A session then I perform a few songs at the end. This has been the most rewarding part of everything that we do: to help show the next generation how much there is to live for and that their goals hold real meaning and are worth fighting for. It has also been very humbling for me as a singer. It's comforting to have them all come on my music journey with me and to have their support for both of us.

We are here today telling you our story because we took a risk in opening up to each other about what we wanted out of life. Connection. Saying the words out loud started an avalanche of possibility and opened us up to growth. Every obstacle we have faced has been an opportunity to learn more about ourselves. Every success has been a reward for living a life true to our hearts' desires.

The name Kada literally popped into my head one night. I wanted a professional name that could represent all that I am. I searched for the meaning of the name and drew a blank; every query, every search engine came back with 'Unknown'. I decided that it was actually perfect because life is so full of unknowns but that's what keeps it interesting. Kada is a reminder to never be afraid to take risks and to let my innate intuition guide me.

Back in 2012 I was fortunate to meet a man named John Edney. He is a friend of Kevin Zinger, and after Kevin showed him my music John offered me a record deal with his independent label, MNO. In the past five years we have recorded an album and released it digitally worldwide, which has been an experience for which I am eternally grateful. I have learnt so much about myself as an artist and what kind of message I want to put out to the world.

I recently started working with a new producer, Mylo Bard from Bird Castle Music Group. His first question to me was, 'Why do you sing?' My answer was: 'I used to want to be a singer simply because I could sing, now I want to be a singer because it is my contribution to the world and this life. I believe that it is our job to use the tools that we have been given to serve the greater good of humanity. My voice is my gift and I want to use it to empower people through my music because music is that powerful. It heals and it brings people together.'

I am really excited about the next part of my music journey. I'm looking forward to exploring my range and constantly pushing the bar in what I can do. As long as I am inspiring myself with the words I write, I will be doing it for the rest of my life.

BARNEY

I've had issues with bladder and kidney stones twice since the first big one. I had surgery the second time around but when another showed up in a scan for the third time, I needed to find the source of what was causing it. We started to work with an integrative doctor, Dr Gull, and an incredible naturopath named Tony who is also a compounding chemist and nutritional bio-chemist. We looked at the stones as a sign to take our journey to the next level and really connect mind, body and soul.

Kada and I both had our genes tested to see the blueprints for our DNA. We learnt what we are susceptible to and what kind of lifestyle is best suited to create the best outcome for our health. We've learnt about epigenetics through podcasts with

Bruce Lipton and Gregg Braden, which show that our genes are influenced by our lifestyle and environment and are like switches we can turn on and off. We had heavy-metal tests done, which showed that we both had high levels of multiple heavy metals. We then did the organic acid tests that detect the bacteria types and levels in the gut. We both had issues with corn; it didn't mean we could no longer have it, just that we needed to make more effort to make sure it was organic. We also each had a full blood panel, which showed the state of our methylation pathways, which as we suspected needed some cleaning up. We were both put on a new program of natural supplements and herbal tinctures and also started to make more conscious choices in what we ate.

After eight months I went for a follow-up appointment to see if the herbs and supplements had made a difference to my stones or if I had to go in for another surgery. It was pretty awesome to hear the urologist say that whatever I was doing to keep it up, the stones were no longer there and all that was left was a bit of sludge that would pass naturally over the next few days. The human body really is so amazing and I can't help but believe that these stones were just another lesson to be learnt and a way to push us into a whole new phase of healing.

When you start to learn the bio-chemistry make-up of the body, you really begin to appreciate on a whole new level just how much of a miracle it is that we are alive. That each organ is doing what it is meant to do at the right moment. So, why do we do everything we can to destroy it? Why do we treat it so badly? Now more than ever we understand the true healing power we all hold within ourselves. For so long I was waiting for the right thing to come along to help me recover, even though I held the answer all along. But, that said, it is all part of the journey.

Now we hope that everything that we have learnt over the years can be shared to help make life a bit easier for someone else. Every person has the power within to achieve greatness.

I now have a great team of people in America and at home in Sawtell. I cannot thank my trainer Josh enough for the strength he has helped me regain. His support and fearless approach to pushing my body has got me to where I am today and it is an honour to work with him and call him a mate. I can now stand on my own, I am able to take small assisted steps and every day I am regaining more control over my entire body.

My trainers at home in Sawtell are Hayley and Regan. They are both physios but unlike any physios I have ever worked with. They are both out-of-the-box thinkers and have each brought their unique skill set into my training regime that has been helping expand it more than ever. I was fortunate to meet Eric Goodman, founder of Foundation Training, and have had the opportunity to work with him on multiple occasions. He has become a great mentor and friend in my life. Clint has also since become certified in Foundation, so it will be great to have that incorporated into my program more regularly.

As you all know, surfing has been a major influence in my life. It is my greatest source of energy and where I go to wash away any doubts that might pop up. Being a contender for a World Title is any young competitive surfer's dream, but I thought that dream had gone with my accident. At the end of 2016 I represented Australia and competed in my first surf contest in seventeen years – the Stance ISA World Adaptive Surfing Championship. I came home with a silver medal for myself in the AS5-Assist division and a copper medal for fourth place for Team Australia out of twenty-two countries. It was a rush being back in the competitive headspace. For seventeen years it was me competing against myself and now I finally got to feed the beast within and let the mongrel out. I'm not going to lie, I was disappointed with second place but it was probably the best thing that could have happened to me. It forced me to ramp up my training and helped me in every aspect of my life. I didn't realise how much I'd missed that life until I got the taste again. In 2017 I requalified for the Australian team after winning the Aussie Title in my division and then took out first place in the US Open Adaptive Surf Championships a few months later. That was a pretty satisfying feeling and definitely scratched the itch, but the real prize I had my eye on was the World Title.

Placing second in the Worlds had been eating at me all year. It lit a flame in me that I hadn't felt in almost two decades. My mate Toby had said to Kada, 'Don't you worry about him, I have seen what happens to Barney when he gets second, he is coming for them all.' He was reminiscing about our competitive days together, but he was right. There was no way I was letting it slip away from me again. That title was mine.

From 29 November to 3 December 2017 I put on the red rashie which is given to the highest seeded surfer of each heat. Then heat by heat I held on to the top spot. I held my winning streak all the way to the final. Finals day arrived and I was more than ready to make everyone who has ever supported me proud and claim that gold medal for my country. To me this was more than a win, it was even more than a World Title. This represented all the years I had fought the statistics and the label I had been given for the previous eighteen years. It was my moment to prove to myself that I have what it takes to achieve any goal I set my mind to.

I paddled out with my main man Dana as my pusher – he helped select the best waves to charge – and Hiddo was my catcher on the inside; he would paddle me back out to the line-up after I caught a wave in. It was mid-tide and the waves turned on. The swell was increasing but not really handling the bigger sets, so we stuck to our game plan of taking on the medium-sized peaks. I was riding my DHD surfboard designed by Darren Handley himself. We have been working together on boards for a few years and this one is a weapon and so responsive to all the manoeuvres I try. I love pushing the limits in everything I do and to me surfing is about self-expression and making it fun to watch. When I surf it is with passion and intent, and thankfully that shone through in the scores. In the final three minutes I had the three other competitors comboed, which meant in order for them to win they needed a combination of two higher scores. I knew it was a long shot but not impossible, so I stayed calm and collected. Then the final thirty-second countdown began and those words I had wanted to hear since I was a young grom echoed across the beach: 'The World Champion . . . Barney Miller.'

Then came tears, screams, fist pumps and Kada running fully clothed into the water with tears falling down her cheeks to give me a hug and a kiss. I was chaired up the beach on my surfboard with Grinspoon's 'Champion' blaring and the whole team chanting along.

I had done it. I'd actually pulled it off.

It was a powerful moment in my life – and the proudest moment to hold the Australian flag while the national anthem played with the gold medal around my neck. I was so honoured to share this win with my boys Dana and Hiddo; we had worked so hard for it.

Australia's blind surfer, Matt Formston, also took gold at the World Championships. Watching him surf still blows my mind. Out of twenty-six countries, Team Australia came home with the overall silver medal. We missed the gold by only 500 points, but we were all so stoked with our efforts and proud to be part of an awesome team.

It all really started to sink in when we arrived home in Australia. We landed in Coffs Harbour with the flight attendant congratulating me on the World Title over the loudspeaker and telling us to look out our windows to see the fire brigade giving the plane a water salute in honour of my gold medal for Australia. As we walked through the doors of the terminal we were greeted by friends and family holding signs and with lots of hugs. Now it's said and done I am prouder than I could ever have thought possible. It was a dream come true and one I can't wait to defend, but not too many times, because next I plan to learn to surf standing up.

It definitely wasn't the journey I had planned for myself but it turned out so much better. I am proud to be an ambassador for adaptive surfing and to be part of a movement that inspires people to just get out there and make it happen, whatever that means for you. I've said it before but the ocean is so healing, it is so energising, and it is such a force that, once you surrender to its power, it will be part of you forever. A surfer's love for the ocean is far greater than any obstacle he or she will ever face because it has the power to make you whole again.

KADA AND BARNEY

Who knows what the future holds for us? All we know is that we will continue to stay open to wherever life takes us. One thing that we are excited about, though, is to start a family. For all you perverts who have been wondering throughout this whole story if we can still Get It On . . . Yes, happy to report that everything is more than good to go in that department. We understand you can never really prepare yourself for how much life will change with kids but we are both dedicated to getting ourselves to optimum health to create a healthy bub and a healthy life for us all. We are also very passionate about adoption too. There are so many beautiful kids out there who all deserve to know and feel love. That is a human right. In our perfect world, Barney will teach them to surf and I will teach them music, but that might not be their thing and that's okay too. As long as they are healthy, happy and experiencing things that they love, then that's all we could ever hope for.

This journey of ours has had many ups and downs, but hasn't everyone's? The greatest lesson we have learnt along the way is that there is always hope. When you are open to love, it will find you in so many beautiful ways and fill your heart with a strength that will help you move mountains. Look for the signs, they are everywhere around you. It's all about perception.

We are so grateful for all the people and our dogs who have been part of our story. We wish we could have told a story of each of you and how you have all had an impact on our lives but you have all helped us in more ways than you will ever know and we thank you from the bottom of our hearts. Someone once told us, life is the hardest thing you will ever do . . . they were not wrong, but as long as we are here, we will keep fighting to make it meaningful. With tragedy we were shown a rainbow and we made a choice to follow it. We found love on the other side and the true meaning of humanity. We found the essence of you and me.

ACKNOWLEDGEMENTS

KADA AND BARNEY

Thank you to our families for the unconditional love and support you have all shown us over the years. It is with your presence in our lives that we have had the courage to push the boundaries of each day.

To our friends – our chosen family – you are the grounding our foundations are built upon and we are so honoured every day to learn from you all. We are who we are because the environment we choose to surround ourselves with is filled with pure love and support.

BARNEY

Mum and Mal, Dad and Sue, Lara and Tahn – thank you for sticking by me through the hardest days of my life. I know I don't say it enough, but I love you and I am the luckiest boy alive to have had you as my family. I honestly could not have gotten through it without you all, and thank God I did, because now I get to be the best uncle to Tristan, Asta, Indica and Ella.

To my step-family – Tommy, Kira, Jake, Josh, Sarah, Jesi, Hannah, Claire and Bonnie – thank you, it was fun growing up with you.

Toby, you have been the best mate I could have ever had. Thank you for pushing me from a young age and sparking my competitive spirit. I have no doubt in my mind that my stubborn fight and my inner mongrel was created with you – you gave him life. Our days of competing in everything that we did has given me strength in everything I do now. It's a reminder of all the things I have to gain if I just keep pushing through. You were always my greatest competition, so thank you for never letting me give up.

And to the Webbers – when Toby became my best friend for life I gained a new family who have been so welcoming and supportive in all that I am. Thank you for being part of my life and allowing me to be part of yours. My life would not be the same without you.

To Mick Fanning, our friend who inspires us every day to simply try. We are here today because of your friendship. After we both told you our goals, you opened the doors to show us they were possible. Your belief in us helped us believe in ourselves, and for that we will always be grateful. Thank you.

To our surfing family, being part of a community that is connected around the world through the love of the ocean is amazing. The support you have given us travels with us wherever we go and brings us the comfort we need whenever things get hard. We are grateful that one day our children will be part of it all. Dana, thanks for getting me motivated to be out in the surf more and for helping make it happen. It is an honour to share my wins with you and I look forward to many more adventures together.

To my sponsors, the brands and the people who encouraged and supported me to just get out and surf – Ripcurl, Dragon Eyewear, GoPro, FCS, Darren Handley DHD Surfboards, Souls, Pitaya Plus, Sun Bum, Poolwerx, Red Bull – I am proud to have you all on my team and to be part of yours. Our partnership is more than a sponsorship, you are part of our journey and your support has given me a purpose to strive for better every day.

KADA

Mum, Dad, Rachael, Brad, Clarissa, Anthony, Nicholas, Zanda, Belle and Daimon – I am so grateful to be part of a family that is loving and kind. You always taught me to see the best in people, thank you. I will never stop believing in your dreams and encouraging greatness in you. Every day I will strive to be the best daughter, big sister and aunty. I love you so much – thank you for loving me, even when you think I'm weird.

Thank you especially to Mum and Dad for your unconditional love and your patience.

To my beautiful girlfriends, thank you for your love and support. To Monique and Gem, you have been my friends the longest. I treasure you both so much and, even though we hardly see each other, I know you are here, and I am there with you for every milestone. Em and Kel, ten years of friendship and it only gets stronger with every day. We have laughed together, cried together and danced together till the music stops and we were made to go home. I want to be doing cocktail hour with you two till the end of time. Christina, I may have gotten you because of Toby but I love you because of yourself. You are my biggest cheerleader and a friend that reminds me to be true to myself and my heart. So actually thanks to Toby for bringing us together!

Jem and Hayley, you may have only been in my life for a short time but you have both made a huge difference to it. My soul feels at home whenever I am in your presence and our shared love of all things holistic inspires me in every conversation.

Bec, thank you for being my 'big sister'. Our family dinners have brought me so much comfort over the years. I will always be grateful to you and Marto for welcoming me into your family.

Bree, my soul sister, there are no coincidences, just destiny. Bree came into my life at Melbourne airport when I dropped my bags all over the road while crossing with Barney. She and her boys came over to help, and as she looked up at me, she told me that they were coming to see our film,

ACKNOWLEDGEMENTS

You and Me, the following night. We saw each other again at the screening and then she brought another friend to the second screening in Melbourne. We have spoken almost every day since. We are more connected than I ever thought possible. We text each other the same thing at the same time! We live eighteen hours apart but it doesn't make a difference. We even share the same eye prescription, which we realised when I recently left my glasses at home and needed to borrow hers! I believe with every fibre of my being that we are meant to do life together. She is the mother of three beautifully wild boys and her grace and the love she has for raising them as boys, but also as such respectful and thoughtful people, inspires me every day. I am eternally thankful for that stressful moment in the middle of the road, bags sprawled out with cars lining up waiting for us to clear the crossing, because now I have a real-life angel to walk through life with.

And to the rest of my gal-pal tribe – Hannah, Son, Trace, Tegan, Nic, Lou, Amy, Tonya, Bec, Amanda, Amie, Erika and Alycia – I love you.

To my sisters-in-law Lara and Tahn, thank you for welcoming me into your family with open arms and treating me as your own. I love you.

I am so blessed to be surrounded by strong empowered women who inspire me in so many ways. Our friends and the ones closest to us are the perfect mirrors. Each person represents a different aspect of who we are in that moment and teaches us more about ourselves.

BARNEY AND KADA

To every single mentor, therapist, trainer, healer, music producer and medical professional who has helped us, you have given us a life of freedom. Our goals may not have been fully reached yet, but right here, right now, we are so proud of who we are and who you have all guided us to be.

Ken and Nickie Ware, Josh Salic, Mica Ramos Gaila, Jason Wanstreet, Laurie McAlister, Jason Smith, Eric Harness, Jan Carton, Clint Greenshields, Eric Goodman, Hayley Reynolds and Regan Wild, Tony Salloon, Dr Gull Herzberg, Rob Kidd, Angie Greenshields, Cindy Currie, Dana Barre, Marta Hotell, Nick, Irene Pachos, Laura Blockley, Genny Kroll-Rosen, Ron W. Rathbun – we thank you.

Mick Lawrence, we shared this story because you gave us the courage to. Your friendship and guidance over the past few years have meant so much to us and given us the most rewarding gift of all: to be authentically ourselves and share it with the world.

Michael Crossland, you have no doubt been one of our greatest inspirations (we only save that word for people who truly embody the definition). The hand you have been dealt and continue to live through proves that the quality of our lives is only a state of mind. You have taken the obstacles that life has thrown at you and, instead of crumbling, transformed those devastating experiences into self-empowering wisdom to share with the world. Thank you to you and Mel for your friendship; we are honoured to share this life with you. (Michael is the author of Number One International Bestseller Kids Don't Get Cancer)

Taylor and Lorenzo, this all started with you, two college film students who believed in sharing a story which could empower people to fight for their dreams and never take no for an answer. Can you believe where it has taken us? We are so grateful to you both for helping us follow our dreams, because along the way we gained a brother and a sister who have given our lives a purpose so much greater than just ourselves.

In 2017 our film, You and Me, *received Surf Video of the Year at the Surfing Australia Awards. After our speech we were congratulated by our wonderful publisher Vanessa Radnidge and Managing Director Louise Sherwin-Stark from Hachette Australia. This was the moment that brought us here. Having the opportunity to share our story through documentary was one of the most rewarding experiences of our lives, and the rawness was the most empowering part of it. It finally gave us permission to lift the veil we had been hiding under and to say to the world, this is us. Writing our story was more challenging than expected. It forced us into a deep place to remember the emotions and reflect on each event in our lives. Thank you, Vanessa, Louise and Publishing Director Fiona Hazard, for this opportunity. This process has been incredibly healing for us both. We learnt so much more about ourselves and one another. So, to anyone who is needing a reminder of how amazing life is, or wants* to get to know themselves a bit better, write about it. Even just for yourself. It is so fulfilling to see where you were and where you are now right there in front of you. Plus, the pages have a unique way of seeking the truth out of you to help you confront your demons.

Thank you to our editors Tom Bailey-Smith, Claire de Medici and the whole team at Hachette. You have been a dream to work with and we are honoured to be telling our story through you. Also, a big thankyou to our sister Lara for helping us with the final edit. Having your honest feedback and sharing this experience with you was so special.

To our Sawtell and Southern California fams, we are so blessed to have an incredible group of friends in both places we call home. Every day we thank our lucky stars for you all.

Jäger and Nitro, our fur babies, you have given us a love we have never known. You fill our hearts and, no questions asked, have always been there for us. You are the most loyal best friends and have made our lives so abundant. There is a saying, 'be the person your dog thinks you are' – well, we will strive every day to be deserving of you and to live by your example, to be present and always live from a place of love. We said goodbye to our beautiful boy Jäger in the last days of editing this book. It is a heartbreak we have never felt before but we are comforted by the eleven years of memories he gave us and the love we shared. He will always be one of the greatest loves of our lives and this book is written in memory of him.

RESOURCES

SPINAL INJURY RECOVERY AND THERAPIES

AUSTRALIA

Making Strides, Burleigh, Queensland
makingstrides.com.au
info@makingstrides.com.au
07 5520 0036

NeuroPhysics Therapy Institute, Burleigh, Queensland
www.neurophysicstherapy.global
info@neurophysicstherapy.global
07 5593 0688

Sunlighten Saunas
sunlighten.com.au
1800 786 544

UNITED STATES OF AMERICA

Strides SCI, San Juan Capistrano, California
stridesci.com
contact@stridessci.com
949 354 5655

Foundation Training
foundationtraining.com

Kelee Meditation
thekelee.org

Sunlighten Saunas
sunlighten.com
877 292 0020

TEN QUICK TIPS TO GET CONNECTED WITH YOURSELF

1. Switch off: put your phone in aeroplane mode, get in nature, journal, exercise any way you can, meditate – these are all great ways to get back in touch with you
2. Move your body
3. Hydrate
4. Do something every day that makes your heart sing
5. Take risks
6. Look in the mirror and tell yourself that you are beautiful and worth loving
7. Say five things you are grateful for every day (after a few days of this practice, we bet you can't stop at five)
8. Dream big
9. Find something that scares you, then do it anyway
10. Share your goals with others.

⬛ @kadamiller
⬛ @barney_miller